A NON-TECHIE BEGINNERS' GUIDE TO CYBERSECURITY AND PRIVACY

HOW ANYONE CAN SECURE THEIR DIGITAL LIFE, PROTECT DATA, AND PREVENT CYBER ATTACKS IN 5 EASY STEPS

TECHED PUBLISHERS

CONTENTS

Part II

SECURING AND PROTECTING YOUR DIGITAL LIFE

Free Cybersecurity Course!

Jumpstart your journey to a safer digital world! Sign up now for our exciting, free course on cybersecurity!

Cybersecurity Unlocked: A 10-Email Masterclass in Cybersecurity Essentials

- Master cybersecurity and safeguard your digital identity with our step-by-step guide!
- Dive into interactive lessons, quizzes, and real-world scenarios
- Gain expert insights on common online threats and practical tools to secure your devices and personal info

To get your free course, please visit the link or scan the QR code below and let us know the email address to send it to.

pages.techedpublishers.com/bonus/cpntu

Don't miss out!

INTRODUCTION

Very few people today can remember a life when, before the invention of TV, the only remote information technology people encountered was the radio or land-line telephone. In the last century, technology has rapidly advanced and continues to do so at an unprecedented rate. Today, technology has crept into every part of our lives. The "connectedness" we experience today is astounding; people have smart home devices, AI-assisted living, and they can message or video call someone on the other side of the world. Furthermore, younger generations are growing up in a digital age where every aspect of their lives is intertwined with technology, from learning to playing. Fewer and fewer adults remember a world where people weren't glued to their mobile devices.

As convenient as this increased connectedness and dependency on technology may be, it has brought new challenges.

Perhaps the most widespread and prominent danger in this increasingly technological world is cybercrime. Crime has existed for as long as society has, but with all this advancement and reliance on the internet, it has drastically evolved. Once upon a time, burglaries struck fear into the hearts of homeowners. Technology came up with solutions to combat the threat and quell the fear; security cameras around people's properties not only deterred would-be burglars but also to catch those in the act if they were indeed brazen enough to ignore the cameras. Now, burglaries are still a worry. However, they were much more at the forefront of people's minds in the past. These days, the same home-owners who installed surveillance cameras to protect them-selves are plagued by the worry that those cameras could be used against them. Cybercriminals hacking into a home surveillance system can effortlessly and secretly spy on unsuspecting residents, listening to private conversations, observing behaviors, and gathering sensitive information.

That is just one example, among many, of how technology has evolved to serve us, but criminals have also adapted to make it serve their nefarious purposes. Every aspect of our interactions with information technology has been exploited by cybercriminals to expose and capitalize on vulnerabilities and opportunities. To make matters even more problematic, cybercrime targets aren't limited to society's financial cream of the crop or to information-rich organizations. Even the average Joe on the street has been assimilated into cyber-crime's seemingly endless supply of potential victims. To put this sobering fact into perspective, there are an average of 97 cybercrime victims every hour worldwide. That's cybercrime successfully occurring every 37 seconds. Even more hair-raising is the statistic that in 2022 alone, the information of 2 internet users was leaked every single second (Griffiths, 2023).

Now, this sounds like predictions of guaranteed doom and gloom for all who have anything to do with information technology. You may even be suddenly weighing up the pros and cons of going off-grid to preserve your sanity and negate the worry of knowing these statistics. This knowledge should certainly be a wake-up call that makes you sit up straight and seriously contemplate your personal cybersecurity. However, as shocking as these figures are, you don't have to retreat from interacting with technology. Information technology is a part of everyday life now, and avoiding it altogether is impossible. So, how do you navigate the digital age we live in and still avoid becoming a cybercrime statistic? Is that even possible?

The answer is a resounding "YES!" It is possible to lead a life where technology is integrated into almost every aspect of it. The best part is that you don't have to be a tech genius to accomplish cybersafety and privacy. Cybersecurity is becoming increasingly crucial for everyday users, like you, your spouse, mother, father, best friend, child, or the person you meet at a café and strike up a conversation with. Effective cybersecurity will require a concerted societal effort, and it's possible to minimize the effects for yourself and those around you... but it starts with you.

You need this step-by-step guide that simply and effortlessly explains the ins and outs of cybersecurity and how to protect yourself. In the first section of this guide, you'll discover:

- What cybersecurity is and why it applies to everybody
- How cybercrime impacts organizations and individuals
- The real-world effects of cybercrime-related in fact-based case studies and reports
- The core fundamentals of a sound cybersecurity strategy
- What the common types of cyberattacks are
- The legal and ethical aspects of cybersecurity, pertinent prominent laws, and the importance of compliance

Once you have a deeper understanding of the theoretical side of cybersecurity, you will be more motivated to implement a practical approach to your personal privacy protection. Thus, the second section of the guide is a systematic, step-by-step guide that will walk you through implementing cybersecurity tools and practices:

- Understanding what essential cybersecurity tools and practices are and why they're necessary so you can have a greater insight into your protection options
- Securing your devices and networks

- Securing your digital accounts and information
- Securing your online browsing and social media
- Making use of cyber hygiene tips and a master checklist for easy reference as you navigate your interactions with technology while maintaining tight personal security measures

Cybersecurity isn't a fad. It's not something that happens to others; it may well happen to you. It's a real threat faced by everyone who lives in our modern age of gadgets and digital connectedness. It is likely, if you haven't already been a victim of cybercrime, that you've probably at least encountered some attempted cyberattacks. It's an unavoidable risk, but you don't have to fall victim. You can and should protect yourself. This guide is specifically designed to easily and efficiently steer everyday users through the potential minefield that is information technology. It takes the confusion out of tech-related jargon. It makes cybersecurity principles and practices accessible and relatable to regular technology users, not just the tech-minded.

It's time to take your personal cybersecurity seriously and increase your protection and privacy. To take the next step and start your journey, all you have to do is keep reading.

PART I

BUILDING A FOUNDATION IN CYBERSECURITY AND PRIVACY

1

UNDERSTANDING THE FUNDAMENTALS OF CYBERSECURITY

Cybersecurity can be a complex topic to tackle. It comprises theoretical understanding and practical application of vital security measures. Before you can genuinely begin implementing better cybersecurity practices, it's imperative to gain a fuller understanding of the theoretical side.

You may question why the theory behind the practices is so critical and why you can't simply implement security measures. Cultivating a cybersecurity mindset is the basis for setting up a thorough security strategy and effectively maintaining it to ensure your security is consistently audited and adapted as the cybercrime threat landscape evolves. That mindset is built on understanding what you're doing and why – it is not just putting security measures in place like a robot. When you better understand the reasoning behind the practices, you're more likely to be consistent with the methods, more vigilant of the human element of cybercrime, and more thorough with your cybersecurity hygiene.

The notion of cybercrime perhaps paints a picture of a hooded figure in a dark room seated behind a brightly lit computer screen, feverishly typing away on a keyboard. You can thank Hollywood for this dramatic caricature of cybercrime and its perpetrators. While cybersecurity focuses on using information technology to commit a wide range of crimes, the technology itself is only part of the concern. Cybercrime has a solid foundation in human nature and behavior, and an effective cybersecurity strategy is just as heavily rooted in the human element of using technology. That is why having a reasonable understanding of cybercrime and how it can affect anybody, not just corporate bigwigs or large organizations, is crucial.

This understanding will likely inject a healthy dose of concern for your personal cybersecurity and increase your motivation to improve your security and privacy. However, you can't just start looking up and implementing security measures willy-nilly. You'll need a structured cybersecurity framework or strategy to work from and determine which security practices to take on board based on that framework.

Finally, cybersecurity is governed by laws, locally, country-wide, and internationally, including defining what information is protected and how it's protected. As an individual, you may not be obligated to comply with many of these laws, as they're primarily aimed at organizations handling peoples' information. However, understanding the ethics of cybersecurity, compliance with the regulations, and what the most prominent laws are gives you deeper insight into your rights as a consumer. You'll also be able to make more informed decisions about choosing information technology products and services based on this new knowledge.

That is what the first section of this guide will be all about. It will lay down critical foundational knowledge of cybercrime and cybersecurity as well as providing a guideline for creating a proper security strategy. From there, you'll be able to more effectively and efficiently navigate your way through implementing the various steps of the cybersecurity guide in the second section.

2

CYBERSECURITY AND PRIVACY BASICS

C an you have privacy without security? Privacy and security can sometimes be mistaken for each other, but they are not necessarily the same thing. In the cyber realm, privacy refers to the regulations and laws that control the protection of your personal information. This applies to all manner of organizations you may come in contact with, from banks to healthcare to social media platforms. Privacy essentially means keeping your sensitive information out of the cyber public eye. Security, on the other hand, is how that information is stored, protected, and accessed, which in turn necessitates technical, physical, and administrative measures for protection. Simply put, it's possible to have security without privacy, but it's not possible to have privacy without security. The next question is, what does this mean to you?

The demand for the general public to be connected to all sorts of devices – and their demand to conduct their business and daily life online – is ever-growing. From the smart-watch on your wrist to the laptop you do your banking on, to the smartphone you connect to both your watch and laptop to transfer information back and forth, technology is an inevitable part of modern life. The fact that you can't have privacy without proper security makes cybersecurity a top priority for anyone who uses a connected device.

WHAT IS CYBERSECURITY, AND WHY IS IT SO IMPORTANT?

Let's break the word down into its most fundamental components. 'Cyber' refers to anything that has to do with computers, devices, information technology, and, of course, the internet. You know what security means, as we've just clarified that part. And we have also explained that privacy is an inherent part of any effective cybersecurity strategy.

Cybersecurity refers to protecting your data, networks, devices, computer systems, and applications for protecting from a cyberattack, as well as recovering information in the event your security is breached. In a world so heavily reliant on technology, nobody is safe from a potential cyberattack.

Cybercriminals will take any available opportunity to steal any information that can benefit them in any possible way. That could mean swindling you out of the last five bucks in your account, impersonating you, or even stealing your identity. These criminals are unscrupulous, and they are not only out to access the bank accounts and private data of wealthy individuals or multinational companies. In fact, they are less likely to take on those cyber users because they usually have very tight security, which makes the job of breaching their devices and accounts more difficult. By targeting people who may not take cybersecurity as seriously or who may need to gain the know-how to protect themselves fully, they're more likely to be successful without having to put in as much work.

In essence, you, your family and friends, neighbors, and even the barista who serves you coffee in the morning are much more appealing potential victims to cybercriminals. Sure, large corporations and organizations still get targeted, but it's the man on the street who is more at risk. That makes cybersecurity vital for anyone who uses any form of technology, irrespective of whether or not you think you have anything of great value to criminals.

WHY IS CYBERCRIME ON THE RISE?

When you think of cybercrime, you may think about the typical Hollywood portrayal of bank accounts being hacked so criminals can lay their hands on tons of money. That's only one aspect of cybercrime. This branch of criminality also includes:

- Stealing a person's identity for criminal purposes
- Stealing information that can be used to commit other crimes

- Compromising data integrity by changing or destroying the information
- Compromising the integrity of a person, organization, or government with the aim of making them seem untrustworthy

Cybercrime is on the increase, and there are a couple of reasons for this:

- Population increase, causing more people to rely on technology to navigate life
- People spend more time using technology and being online
- An increasing number of businesses and organizations are storing the personal information of the people they deal with online on cloud services
- The internet is an incredibly distributed system with a vast number of "moving parts", such as devices, computers, and networks. The more parts there are to a system, the more vulnerable it can be
- Cybercrime is much harder to police than local crimes committed in person because criminals can perpetrate attacks from far outside the jurisdiction where the crime is being executed
- The increasing sophistication of the technology helps cybercriminals conduct their unsavory business more easily on the 'dark' web
- The difficulty of policing cybercrime ramps up its popularity and profitability. Criminals are putting

less on the line and gaining more.

WHAT IMPACT DOES CYBERCRIME HAVE?

This question has two answers. Cybercrime impacts both businesses and the lives of individuals, both of which can be disastrous.

The impact of cybercrime on business includes:

- Financial losses incurred when intellectual property is stolen, damaged systems (which must be repaired), trading or business activity being disrupted, or corporate information becoming compromised
- Damage to reputation when consumer trust is lost, which in turn leads to the loss of both current and future consumers to competitors with better security reputations
- The three-fold cost of implementing security systems to conform to data protection regulations, training personnel to be cybersecurity-aware, and hiring cybersecurity personnel
- Potential fines or sanctions for not adhering to the regulations or as a result of falling victim to cybercrime

It's quite possible that a lack of cybersecurity could destroy your business, but what about individual people? How are they affected? The impact of cybercrime on individuals is far-reaching and includes:

- Financial loss incurred when financial information, such as banking details and credit card details, are stolen
- Financial loss incurred through identity theft, where the person's identity is used to take out loans or credit
- Reputational loss from cyberbullying, identity theft, and impersonation
- Mental and emotional distress or trauma caused by the crimes and dealing with their repercussions

For both businesses and individuals, the impact of cyber-crime can be devastating. Due to the anonymous nature of many of these crimes, the perpetrator can disappear without a trace, never suffer any consequences, and it can take years for the victim to recover, if they ever do.

CORE CYBERSECURITY FUNDAMENTALS

Cybersecurity strategies are typically referred to as frame-works for business and enterprise. A cybersecurity frame-work is a set of guidelines, standards, and practices that help manage your cyber risks, similar to a rulebook. Its purpose is to provide an information technology user with a systemic approach to lowering their chances of cybersecurity breaches and how to handle an attack if one happens. Organizations are usually obligated to have a security framework as it ensures that they comply with local, industry, and international cybersecurity laws, but everyday users aren't. However, having a framework in place for your personal cybersecurity is a good idea. It could be a valuable tool for improving and maintaining your information security.

Cybersecurity frameworks are designed to:

- Identify potential security threats
- Protect against possible attacks
- Detect breaches when they happen
- Respond swiftly and accordingly to an attack to minimize its impact
- Aid the recovery from any damage to systems caused by a cybersecurity attack

The five fundamental principles within a cybersecurity framework which can be applied to everyday users are:

Identify Threats

This is the skill of identifying where your potential weaknesses lie, rather than identifying potential attacks or cyber-crime activity itself. Where can cybercriminals infiltrate your privacy? Identify all cyber-related technology you use, including software applications and hardware like computers, laptops, tablets, smartphones, and broadband routers. You'll also need to identify all the sensitive data you use and where you use it.

Protect Information

Information protection is the preventative step of cybersecurity and is your first line of defense against attack. Protecting information involves:

- Physically controlling who has access to your devices.
- Monitoring the activity and details of any device, system, or network you use
- Employing security software
- Regularly updating your security software
- Regularly backing up data
- Educating yourself (and anyone who has access to your devices, systems, or networks) about cybersecurity and about the measures to be put in place to protect your data

Detect Security Breaches

Just because you have cybersecurity measures in place doesn't mean you're now automatically safe from attack. To say cybercriminals are cunning and underhanded is an understatement. The tactics they use to perpetrate their crimes are continually evolving to adapt to new technology, developments in cybersecurity, in their bid to be more successful at spinning a profit from their crimes. Therefore, no preventative security measures are innately indefinitely infallible, which means you will need to be vigilant. Keeping your guard up to detect cybersecurity breaches involves:

- Keeping an eye out for any unauthorized access to your devices, systems, or networks, which may include access via software, hardware (like USB), or logins

- Being vigilant of unauthorized connections to your devices – this is especially important in an era of wireless connectivity to surrounding networks and devices
- Looking into any activity on your devices, systems, or networks that seems unusual or suspicious. This is particularly vital if you allow others access to them

Respond to Security Breaches

"Hope for the best and be prepared for the worst" – Maya Angelou.

You should take this quote to heart when it comes to cyber-security. You are not being negative or pessimistic but rather realistic. You are being a realist because the risk of a security breach, irrespective of your preventative measures, is a genuine threat. So, part of your cybersecurity strategy should be preparedness in the event of a breach. Being prepared in case of an attack means being prepared to do the following:

- Notify anybody you are connected to through technology about the attack because their data may be at risk now, too
- Know how to keep your life or business running smoothly while you are dealing with the security breach

- File a report of the attack with various applicable local authorities.
- Seek the assistance you'll enlist to investigate the attack
- Knowhow to contain the attack to minimize damage
- Deal with unforeseen circumstances which could put your information at risk, such as harsh weather

Finally, responding to a security breach also means learning from the experience and using the knowledge you've gained to improve and update your security measures.

Recover After a Security Breach

Once you've contained an attack and prevented cybercriminals from re-accessing your information, it's time to recover from the event. This step in the process can take on many forms, depending on what damage the attack did and whether you are a business or an individual.

For a business, recovery may include:

- Repairing and restoring networks and systems that have been affected
- Repairing and restoring or replacing devices that have been affected
- Navigating any legal ramifications, such as lawsuits or pursuing legal action against the cybercriminal
- Informing employees and consumers of the steps you've taken to respond to and recover from the event

As an individual, your recovery steps may look very similar to that of a business but may also include:

- Seeking support during your recovery process, which may mean legal advice or the support of family and friends
- Looking after your mental and emotional wellbeing
- Educating yourself further about cybersecurity and implementing new measures you may not have used before
- Reminding your cyber contacts that they need to be vigilant in case any stolen information resurfaces or is used later down the line

UNDERSTANDING THE THREAT LANDSCAPE

Cybercrime comes in all shapes and forms, and not all of them conform to the typical notion of hacking. There are so many types of cybersecurity breaches that an entire book could be written about those alone.

The cybersecurity threat landscape is determined by several factors. The main factors are security vulnerabilities, specific cybercriminals, and attack methods such as malware. Additional landscape components apply to the potential victim and include, but are not limited to, valuable information the victim possesses, the level of their security, and political motivation based on geographic location.

The threat landscape a particular potential target faces is dynamic. It can change based on the evolution of cybercrime or changes to the target. Here are some things that can influence a target's threat landscape:

- Software updates that include new features or functionality
- Security vulnerabilities being discovered which offer unique opportunities for attack
- New hardware platforms being developed
- Changes to the way data is processed
- Significant events with a global influence that cause organizations to alter their infrastructure to accommodate the effects of the event (such as the COVID-19 pandemic)

Understanding your threat landscape is vital to your cybersecurity. It allows you to become aware of the potential threats you face. It enables you to improve or increase security measures to prevent possible attacks and breaches. Part of understanding the threat landscape is knowing what the common types of cybersecurity attacks are, and so you can be wary of them.

COMMON TYPES OF CYBERSECURITY ATTACKS

Code Injection

Code injection attacks involve pieces of malicious code being inserted into an application, such as a website. The code is interpreted by the application, and the functionality of it changes as a result. There are three common types of code injection attacks:

XSS or cross-site scripting: A legitimate application is injected with code that activates on the application user's browser to give the cybercriminal access to the user's sensitive information or allow them to impersonate the user. XSS attacks commonly target applications that enable users to generate their own content, such as message boards and forums. These attacks predominantly take place on the user-facing side of a website or application, where end-users engage and interact.

Malvertising: This occurs when malicious code is inserted into legitimate advertisements, such as banners or display ads, by compromising a third-party server. When a visitor clicks on the ad, the injected code secretly installs malware or adware on their device, posing a security threat.

SQL injection: Database-driven applications use a common computing language called Structured Query Language, or SQL. SQL injection attacks target database-driven applications using SQL. The attack manipulates user queries to gain unauthorized access to the database, enabling the attacker to extract sensitive information, alter data, delete records, or even execute administrative commands like system shutdown. It primarily focuses on the back-end or server-side of a website or application, where end-users don't usually directly interact.

Denial of Service (DOS)

Denial of Service (DoS) attacks target applications or networks that need to handle every user request. The goal is to overwhelm the victim system by flooding it with a massive number of false requests, causing the system to become unable to respond to genuine user or client requests. In some cases, the system's resources become so overloaded that it completely shuts down.

Eavesdropping

An eavesdropping attack is very similar to eavesdropping in day-to-day life. A cybercriminal exploits a vulnerable network, such as an unsecured WiFi network, to intercept messages sent via connected devices. These attacks are sometimes also called "sniffing" or "snooping". They can be used to gather sensitive data such as usernames, account passwords, or even credit card details. There are two types of eavesdropping attacks:

Passive eavesdropping: The criminal inserts software into the network pathway carrying messages and information between users. The software collects information for the attacker.

Active eavesdropping: The criminal does the dirty work themselves, watching the data being transferred across the network to any potentially useful information.

Eavesdropping attacks can also be called man-in-the-middle (MITM) attacks because the attacker places themselves or their software in between the line of communication between two users.

Identity-Based Attack

Cybercriminals are capable of effectively impersonating a legitimate user on an application, system, or network. They gain the credentials of a valid user and then use those credentials for their own gain. Essentially, they're using a legitimate user's information, such as passwords and usernames, which can be difficult for the victim's system to detect as fraudulent activity.

Internet of Things (IoT) Attack

Internet of Things (IoT) refers to all the physical devices that can and are connected to the internet. This creates a global network of interconnected devices linked together by the internet. IoT attacks target devices or networks connected to the internet. Once in, they can further attack other linked devices and systems. The attacks may aim to steal sensitive information or even take control of the device or network. Due to the vast nature of the IoT, a massive array of physical devices can be targeted, including but not limited to computers, smartphones, smartwatches, and smart home devices.

Malware

The term "malware" combines the words malicious and software. It refers to software designed to infect a device, system, or network to steal data, destroy information, alter how an application or device functions, render it inoperable, or spy on users. Cybercriminals are creative with malware, and it can either stay in one place, only affecting a single device or network, or it can replicate and spread to other connected user devices or even across the internet. There are several types of malware, including:

Adware: This form of malware doesn't inherently come with ill intent. It's designed to track your activity to determine which ads to show you. It can, however, degrade your device's performance and impact its usability.

Exploits: Vulnerabilities in a device's operating system or an application are found, and the door is opened for attackers to access a user's data or insert additional malware.

Keyloggers: The software records every keystroke on a device, sending the information back to the attacker, who can then garner all sorts of information from private texts to passwords, usernames, and even banking details.

Ransomware: Malware that encrypts and holds a user's information hostage until a ransom is paid to get it back.

Scareware: Attackers use scare tactics, usually in the form of a pop-up warning, informing users their device is infected and encouraging users to download malware disguised as an antivirus.

Spyware: Information about your online activity is collected without your knowledge.

Trojan: Named after the Greek Trojan Horse, this malware is disguised as or is hidden within legitimate or seemingly harmless files like native operating system programs or free downloads.

Password

Password attacks can take many forms, from snooping through someone's paperwork to see if they've written down their password somewhere to employing code and software. An increasingly popular way of convincing someone to hand over their password willingly is social engineering.

Social engineering attacks often come from seemingly legitimate sources. The cybercriminal impersonates someone trustworthy and attempts to get the victim to supply them with their password or a one-time PIN (OTP) to gain access to their account. This can happen across a wide range of accounts, including banking, mobile service providers, or virtually any account that uses a password to access it. Passwords may also be stolen through eavesdropping, brute force, password spraying, keyloggers, and various other means.

Phishing

Phishing employs a barrage of social engineering techniques to either elicit sensitive information from a victim or convince them to download malware to access the data. Common types of phishing attacks include:

Spear phishing: Individuals or specific organizations are targeted singly in an attempt to gain information or infect a device, network, or system with malware.

SMiShing: These phishing attacks utilize mobile messaging instead of email or phone calls.

Whaling: Also known as whale phishing, these attacks are similar to spear phishing, but they're aimed particularly at high-ranking executives or stakeholders within a company or organization.

Vishing: Instead of emails or text messages, attackers use phone calls or voice messages, impersonate a trustworthy or reputable person or organization, and attempt to convince victims to divulge information such as banking details, passwords, or OTPs.

Spoofing

Spoofing covers a wide range of cyber attacks. The basic principle is the victim is tricked into believing something that isn't true to gain their confidence and ultimately lead them to reveal sensitive information. Some common forms of spoofing include:

Caller ID spoofing: Your caller ID is fooled into showing the call is coming from somewhere it's not. This can include labeling the caller as a legitimate organization or spoofing the area code to make the call seem local in origin.

Email spoofing: Emails are sent from the attacker using a false sender address as part of phishing attacks or attempts to infect the device or network with malware.

Text message spoofing: Similar to caller ID spoofing, text messages use a false phone number or sender ID. These messages can even be sent from laptops and typically employ phishing tactics or downloadable malware.

Website spoofing: A malicious site is made to look like a legitimate website to make you think you are logging into one you frequent only to provide the attacker with your login credentials without your knowledge or consent.

Exploitation

Cyber exploitation happens when intimate images or videos of a victim are distributed without their consent. This type of cybercrime disproportionately targets women and has the potential to do serious harm to the target. A victim of this kind of attack risks damage to their reputation, personal life, and career. The attacker may or may not demand a "ransom" for not distributing the materials, depending on whether they're after financial gain or just out to cause malicious harm.

Swatting

Swatting isn't a new concept. It's based on prank calls to emergency services, but its sophistication and impact have grown over the past years. Instigators of this kind of crime have become more adept at convincing emergency services the threat or situation being reported is real and at targeting specific types of response units to be deployed. While swatting isn't your typical type of cyberattack, it's still worth knowing about. Perpetrators use a variety of methods to gather the necessary information about their victims and to pull the wool over law enforcement's eyes. The aim of swatting is to report a significant crime, such as an active shooter or hostage situation, indicating that the victim of the attack is the person committing the crime. This tactic is used to harass victims, whether they are local to the attacker or located across the country. It's become a popular "prank" among streamers where the attacker summons law enforcement to a streamer's location in hopes of the ensuing chaos being caught on the live stream. Victims can experience multiple swatting instances. They range from a scary encounter with a SWAT team to potentially deadly situations, as was the case when Andrew Finch was erroneously shot and killed during a swatting incident in 2017 (Lynch & Hanna, 2019). Attackers can garner critical information about their targets through social media and other online platforms where personal information is listed.

THE EFFECTS OF CYBERCRIME ON THE REAL WORD

The hold technology has over our daily lives is constantly strengthening, and along with it, cybercrime is continually on the increase. In the 21st century, cyberattacks have made headlines and left not just those directly affected but the entire global online community reeling in their wake. Some of the most notorious cybercrime cases help illustrate the crucial necessity for both organizations and individuals to take cybersecurity seriously. Let's look at some of the most jaw-dropping statistics around cybercrime so far.

2013: Yahoo! Sets a World Record

When Russian hackers set their sights on Yahoo! in 2013, nobody could have predicted the repercussions to the public would drag on for an astounding three years. The cyber-criminals targeted the web service provider's user database in order to access records, including incredibly sensitive personally identifiable information (PII), such as:

- Names
- Birth dates
- Phone numbers
- Email addresses
- Calendars
- Passwords
- Security questions and answers

It was finally estimated that a whopping total of over 3 billion user accounts were affected during this siege. If that's not bad enough, Yahoo! also got into hot water for their slow reaction time and failure to disclose one of the attacks in 2014, attracting 41 class-action lawsuits and costing them $35 million (Chin, 2023).

2013: Adobe Learns a Lesson About Cybersecurity

Adobe is a leading product and service provider for various individual people across many countries and companies. In

2013, the organization came under attack, and the breach has been one of the worst of the 21st century. Information stolen by cybercriminals included more than just names, user IDs, and passwords; the attackers also accessed sensitive payment card details from around 38 million user accounts. The information was posted on the dark web, where other cybercriminals could easily access it for their nefarious purposes (Chin, 2023).

2018 and 2019: Aadhaar and Alibaba Expose Billions of Pieces of User Data

Aadhaar is one of the world's largest ID databases servicing native and foreign national residents within India. In 2018, cybercriminals hacked into the database, obtaining crucial information pertaining to more than 1.1 billion Indian citizens. The information stolen included:

- Identification numbers
- Names
- Biometric data like iris scans and fingerprints
- Phone numbers
- Email addresses
- Physical addresses
- Photographs

The cybercriminals sold off the stolen information, allowing other people and parties to use it for a variety of crimes.

The Chinese shopping website Alibaba suffered a similar blow in 2019 when its database was compromised and data extracted using search and indexing software. The information gained included user names and mobile phone numbers (Hill & Swinhoe, 2022).

2019 to 2021: Facebook Faces Years-Long Data Breach Debacle

In 2019 and again in 2021, Facebook came under fire for a severe data breach that spanned more than two years in the making. It came to light in 2019 that two Facebook-related datasets were publicly exposed to the internet. The exposed information affected more than 530 million Facebook users utilizing the platform between 2018 and 2019. The platform was dealt a second blow in 2021 when, two years later, the stolen data was released for free to all and sundry who would want to access it, including on the dark web. Information leaked included Facebook users' account names, Facebook IDs, and phone numbers (Hill & Swinhoe, 2022).

2021: Microsoft Experiences One of the Largest Attacks in U.S. History

Microsoft Exchange email is one of the world's largest email servers. Unauthorized access due to security vulnerabilities allowed cybercriminals to infiltrate and control the servers. The attack turned Microsoft's servers against itself and its users, fooling many because the requests and contacts came from the Exchange servers, not an external source. According to reports, this cyber attack affected a total of 30,000 companies in the United States and 60,000 companies globally (Chin, 2023).

2021: LinkedIn Loses Face

Many professionals turn to the networking behemoth LinkedIn for a variety of career-related benefits, such as networking, advertising, and advancement. In 2021, though, the platform lost face in a big way when more than 90% of its users were affected by a data breach. Information about more than 700 million people was leaked and threatened to be sold on the dark web. A sample of the stolen information was posted by the hacker and allegedly included:

- Phone numbers
- Email addresses
- Genders
- Geolocation records
- Social media details

(Hill & Swinhoe, 2022)

2022: Large-Scale Data Breaches Are on the Rise Down Under

Cybercrime leading to data breaches, predominantly in the finance and health sectors in Australia, is on the rise. During the second half of 2022, there were around 40 large-scale breaches alone. If that isn't bad enough, the total number of data breaches of varying sizes for that period is in the region of 497 incidents. Of the total number of data breaches in the second half of the year, 75% is being blamed on malicious cybercriminal activity (Tran, 2023).

2022: T-Mobile Is Targeted and Loses Millions

Telecommunications giant, T-Mobile, was hit hard by a widely publicized cyber attack that led to an immense data breach. The personal information of more than 100 million of their customers was compromised. This security breach cost the company a whopping USD 350 million in customer payouts in 2022 (Drapkin, 2023).

2020 to Present: The Growing Threat of RaaS Has Extorted $91Million

Cybercriminals aren't just actively trying to exploit cybersecurity vulnerabilities to extort money or pilfer personal information. There are also those who are simply putting their skills to use by creating and selling malware for other criminals to use. This is where ransomware-as-a-service, RaaS, comes in. LockBit is a RaaS operation that has earned notoriety for extorting $91 million from U.S. organizations through 1700 attacks since 2020. At least 576 organizations were bit by LockBit attacks in 2022. The operation garners profits from ransom payouts its users receive from their victims. This kind of service opens the door for inexperienced criminals who lack the expertise to pull off the attacks to enter the cybercrime scene (Greenberg, 2023).

CYBERSECURITY QUESTIONNAIRE

As you can see from the data breach examples above, some of which were among the worst cases ever encountered, cybersecurity is of vital concern to anyone and everyone who has access to technology. We're sure this chapter has given you some food for thought, but now it's time to ask yourself some crucial questions about how you interact with technology and the IoT.

This questionnaire will help assist you in reflecting on your personal cybersecurity preparedness to assess how well you're really protecting yourself from either deliberately targeted or opportunistic attacks. Take the time to answer these questions in as much detail as you can and be completely honest, so you get the whole picture of the potential risk of a cyber attack.

Identifying Threats

1. What are your potential cybersecurity threats?
2. Refer back to the core fundamentals of cybersecurity covered earlier in the chapter to help identify where and what your risks are.
3. What information technology or devices do you use, both personally and for work?
4. Include absolutely everything from smartphones and other smart devices to computers, card machines, software programs, applications, websites, online shopping portals, and more.
5. What sensitive information do you use or do you have stored on any IT items?
6. Include payment card details, automatic logins, personal information, and more.

Protecting Information

1. What security measures do you employ?
2. Please write these measures next to each IT item you listed in the previous section (i.e., 'Identifying Threats', Question 2's answer).
3. Include passwords, biometrics, and more.
4. How do you keep your account credentials secured?
5. Think about where and how you store login information like user IDs and passwords.
6. Who, aside from you, has access to the devices and software or applications you use?
7. Think carefully about shared devices, such as work computers, shared passwords, and even if you ever leave a device or program logged in and unattended (even around friends and family).
8. Do you protect your devices with security software, such as an antivirus program?
9. It's worth noting that security software differs from using passwords or biometrics to control physical access to a device or account.
10. If you do use security software, do you regularly update it?
11. Do you have vital or sensitive information backed up?
12. Securely and regularly backing up your important information can be a lifesaver in case of a data breach where it can be destroyed or altered maliciously.

Detection and Recovery

1. Do you ever monitor the activity on your devices or accounts?
2. If you do, how do you do it, and how often?
3. Actively monitoring activity will help you detect a security breach more quickly.
4. How will you detect or prevent a cybersecurity breach or attack?
5. This is where monitoring activity comes in handy, but it also helps increase your awareness of potential attacks and be more vigilant.
6. Have you ever encountered cybersecurity attacks or suffered a security breach?
7. These can be phishing emails to social engineering exploits over the phone or even clicking on a link or website your antivirus blocks due to the potential of a threat. Look back on the most common cyber attacks and think about whether you've ever experienced any of them, whether they were successful or not.
8. Do you have a recovery plan in place in case of a security breach?
9. Having a recovery plan in place can have a significant impact on minimizing the damage of a security breach. It can help you maintain focus, de-escalate panic, and allow you to proceed with a level head and confidence.

WHAT'S NEXT?

The extent to which information technology and the internet play a part in our lives is ever-increasing. Many of us may be unable to imagine a world without all these gadgets, or to experience a world where we are not connected to each other via phone or the internet. The more we rely on technology, the more vital cybersecurity becomes. It's no longer just for organizations. Everyday users need to cultivate a cybersecurity mindset. People with low incomes are just as visible to the cybercriminal. It's not always about your bank balance; other sensitive information can be just as alluring to these criminals. You now have a better understanding of what cybersecurity is and how it can impact literally anyone. The next step is understanding what the ethics and legalities of cybersecurity are. This involves how and why organizations are obligated to protect your privacy, and how these same obligations can be directed to everyday users in terms of the organizations' responsibilities to the people around them.

3

ETHICAL AND LEGAL ASPECTS OF CYBERSECURITY

A ny organization that handles any form of personal information pertaining to its clients has an ethical obligation to those clients. This ethical obligation isn't intended to solely protect clients but also to uphold the reputation and functionality of the organization itself. After all, who will trust an organization that cannot or will not adequately protect its own sensitive information? In addition to organizations, individuals should consider their ethical obligations to those they interact with. Many of the same principles that apply to organizations can also apply to individuals, even if they're not legally required to abide by them.

There are two protection obligations organizations have:

1. Protect sensitive information, thereby preventing harm to an individual, group, or organization's

privacy.

2. Protect the intellectual, digital, or physical property of an individual, group, or organization.

In addition to the obligation to protect an individual, group, or organization's privacy and property, organizations (and even individuals) have two additional ethical issues to navigate:

1. They need to weigh up the costs of implementing a cybersecurity system versus the resources they have available. Essentially, they need to consider what their system resources are versus the cost of potential security breaches should the system not be secure enough to thwart attempted attacks.
2. They need to be transparent with the individuals, groups, or organizations they deal with about security vulnerabilities and disclose breaches if they happen.

THE ETHICS OF CYBERSECURITY

Once you understand the ethical obligations organizations are under and individuals should seriously consider, it's time to look at compliance. In adhering to these obligations, additional ethical considerations also come into play. These include:

Service providers: Third-party services range from security software and cloud services to mobile device managers, file sharing, and email. Many of these providers have access to their clients' information, whether those clients are organizations or individuals. Organizations may consider in-house solutions for these services, cutting out the third party altogether. Individuals, on the other hand, usually can't create their own software or other services; individuals therefore have to use third-party providers. It's crucial to investigate and carefully pick any third-party supplier by asking several pertinent questions:

- What security measures do the providers use to safeguard clients' information, such as physical facility protection and encryption of digital information and communications?
- What is the possibility of these providers or their employees keeping, using, or selling any of your information and what are the possible ramifications if they do?
- What policies do they have about law enforcement or the government accessing your data?
- How transparent are they about their security measures and data breaches when they happen?

Security on both ends: In communication, there are two parties involved. It's a two-way street with two endpoints. Organizations are obligated to make sure their end of the communication is secure, but what about the other end? The same applies to your communication with others, including individuals, groups, and organizations. You could have tight cybersecurity measures on your devices, systems, and networks, but that doesn't mean the person or organization you are communicating with has the same.

Cybersecurity Compliance (and Its Importance, and Its Benefits)

Cybersecurity compliance means following the regulations and standards for cybersecurity protocols set by an authority. This authority can be law enforcement, government, or another organization. Generally speaking, compliance is aimed at organizations, not individuals. However, understanding the ins and outs of compliance allows individuals to understand their rights as consumers. For organizations, compliance involves implementing security controls to protect information confidentiality, integrity, and availability, or CIA for shot – not to be mistaken for the U.S. Central Intelligence Agency. These controls don't only apply to stored information but also to sending and receiving it.

Data security is crucial for organizations across the board. It can even play a part in their overall success or failure. No organization worldwide is free from the risk of cyberattacks or security breaches. A data breach can be disastrous for an organization, leading to reputational and financial damages from which they face the possibility of never fully recovering. The benefits of complying with applicable cybersecurity standards and regulations include:

- Identifying and preparing for any potential breaches
- Improved security in general

- Maintaining the organization's reputation
- Building confidence with consumers to improve loyalty
- Building and maintaining consumer trust

Additionally, an organization's cybersecurity compliance ensures your data is secure, and your privacy is protected, shielding you from the potential fallout of having that data stolen.

Types of Protected Data

There are three main types of data protected under cybersecurity laws, namely personally identifiable information (PII), protected health information (PHI), and financial information. Specific examples of data that fall under these three categories include:

PII:

- Address
- Date of birth
- First and last names
- Mother's maiden name
- Social Security Number (SSN)

PHI:

- Appointment history
- Hospital admission records
- Insurance records

- Medical history
- Prescription records

Financial information:

- Bank account information
- Credit card numbers, card verification values (CVV), and expiration dates
- Credit history or credit ratings
- Debit or credit card personal identification numbers (PINs)

Aside from these main categories, other kinds of sensitive data fall within compliance laws, including:

- Biometric data
- Email addresses, usernames and passwords
- IP addresses
- Marital status
- Race
- Religion

Important note: While you, as an individual, are not held responsible for cybersecurity compliance, it's worthwhile taking a moment to think about the potential consequences of a data breach happening to you. What kind of sensitive information pertaining to others do you possess, and what would the ramifications to them be if the information was leaked.

Prominent Cybersecurity Laws

Different geographic locations have other cybersecurity laws. Even within the United States, laws aren't only federal but can also vary by state. Understanding the basics of the most prominent cybersecurity regulations locally and internationally provides greater insight and understanding of your rights as a consumer.

United States

Depending on the state an organization is located in, what industry it operates in, and the type of data storage it uses, an organization is required to comply with several regulations. For example:

- The collecting and handling of financial data is regulated by the Gramm-Leach Bliley Act or GLBA.
- The processing and handling of credit card payment information if regulated by the Payment Card Industry Data Security Standard or PCI DSS.
- A patient's health information is protected by the Health Insurance Portability and Accountability Act, or HIPPA. This federal law also extends to providers offering health care services cloud-based data storage.
- The National Institute of Standards and Technology (NIST) Framework provides regulations for how government agencies tackle cybersecurity.

European Union

While there are several data privacy laws in the European Union, the most important one to know about is the General Data Protection Regulation or GDPR. This regulation lays down the law for the collection, processing, and storage of personal information. Some of the standards within the GDPR include:

- Having protocols in place in the event of a data breach and how it's responded to
- Transparency about the methods of collecting and storing information and how the data is used
- Not keeping data for longer than necessary

United Kingdom

The U.K. has a similar framework to NIST in the U.S., called Cyber Essentials. It provides organizations with expected cybersecurity standards and is backed by the government. Any organization wishing to do business with the government must be certified for Cyber Essentials.

The second prominent set of regulations is the Data Protection Act or DPA. This act provides regulations that govern a wide range of cybersecurity standards, including:

- How data are processed
- Transparency about data handling
- Unauthorized access prevention
- Handling of data breaches

- Disposal of data to maintain security
- Providing consumers with a means to delete their personal information

LEGAL, OR ETHICAL HACKING

The moment you hear the terms "hacker" or "hacking," your mind probably jumps to the conclusion that the person or action is inherently criminal. After all, a hacker is typically considered someone who uses information technology to gain access to information, devices, systems, or networks they are not authorized to access; hacking is the act of doing just that. However, there is such a thing as an ethical hacker.

Ethical hackers are also known as "white hats", and they are essentially authorized and paid to do the same things cyber-criminals do, but for the purposes of cybersecurity and law enforcement. They are cybersecurity experts who are contracted to replicate the same attacks criminal hackers use with the intent to pinpoint an organization's security vulner-abilities. They may target devices, systems, networks, software, or applications. These experts work within an ethical framework of protocols, including:

- **Legally consented activity and intent:** Ethical hackers must always be granted appropriate authorization before they begin hacking.
- **A confirmed clear scope of activity:** What an ethical hacker can do during security assessments is

always clearly defined. They remain within these clearly defined boundaries.

- **The reporting of all vulnerabilities:** Ethical hackers leave nothing out of their assessment report, and they'll even offer advice for fixing any security holes.
- **Adherence to data sensitivity policies:** Ethical hackers understand the nature of data sensitivity and may have to sign non-disclosure agreements. They will also never talk shop to others and reveal any information about their work or clients, which could compromise their integrity.

The most obvious and glaring difference between criminal and ethical hackers is that "white hats" perform legal work to help organizations improve their cybersecurity. In contrast, criminal hackers use their skills to break the law and cause damage.

Bug Bounty Programs

While bug bounty programs, also called vulnerability rewards programs (VRP), aren't strictly ethical hacking programs. They're crowdsourcing efforts which organizations take advantage of, in order to supplement their cybersecurity testing and maintenance. These programs essentially turn regular people into digital bounty hunters. They look for, discover, and report bugs, especially concerning security, in return for a reward.

PROTECTING INTELLECTUAL PROPERTY

The internet is populated with all sorts of media, from images to text. Much of this is referred to as intellectual property. Intellectual property relates to anything that is created from the mind or is a result of someone's creativity, which is a pretty broad array of artefacts and products both tangible and virtual, and includes:

- Art
- Images
- Videos
- Course content
- Educational or informational resources
- Product designs and appearances
- Names, titles, catchphrases
- Symbols and designs
- Inventions

These creations can be owned by either individuals or organizations. With the ever-expanding IoT, it's becoming increasingly important to consider ways to protect your intellectual property.

Why Protect Intellectual Property?

Intellectual property protection is for more than just businesses. It should be a concern for individuals as well. Still, you may wonder why protecting intellectual property is vital, whether it is hobby art, photographs, or anything else.

Some of the benefits of protecting your creations, primarily online will include:

Generating income: Intellectual property can be used to create an income by building a business as your principal source of income or a side hustle. Protecting your creations ensures legal security for building a business or brand, competitive advantage, customer loyalty, and the ability to raise capital. All of this increases the security of being able to generate an income from your intellectual property.

Raising capital: Intellectual property can be an asset, like owning land or other valuable assets. As such, you can raise the capital needed to grow your business or brand by offering intellectual property rights as security against the funds.

Legal security: Having your intellectual property approved for use by any potential business or enterprise in the future secures your ability to develop a business using your creations. It also prevents accidentally infringing on another individual or organization's rights, thus avoiding legal repercussions. It also puts you in a favorable position to take legal action if someone else appropriates your creations to pass off as their own.

Competitive advantage: Intellectual property is usually unique and offers an individual or organization a competitive advantage over their peers in the same field or industry. Protecting that advantage prevents your creations from being stolen and your competitive edge from being compromised.

Customer loyalty: Producing creations that customers are attracted to is a massive advantage for the security of your blossoming business. Protecting that intellectual property may help prevent competitors from copying your creations and stealing your customers.

Types of Intellectual Property Protection

Just like there are different types of intellectual property, there are different types of protection. The type of protection you choose may be decided by the type of property you want to protect. Here's the low-down on other ways to protect your creations:

Copyright: This is usually indicated by the copyright symbol, ©, but you don't necessarily have to use it to maintain your rights. You don't have to apply for this form of protection either. It's automatically granted to the creator of any intellectual property the moment it's created. As such, the copyright for anything belongs to the original creator unless a specific, legally binding contract has been entered into, transferring the rights to a new owner. This is vital if you have a business and outsource certain aspects, such as logo creation. The individual or organization who created the work retains the copyright of that work unless the right is legally handed over. This includes writers, photographers, and much more, making it crucial to obtain the rights to any vital work done for your business.

Trademark: A trademark is intended to protect commercial intellectual property and identify where a product or service originally comes from. Original work is inherently copyright protected, but you cannot legally sue in defense of trademark infringement unless you have registered the trademark. A trademark can be any of the following:

- Name
- Word
- Slogan
- Phrase
- Logo
- Symbol
- Sound

Design registration: This form of protection applies to design aspects of products, whether they are physical or digital. How the product looks, functions, or feels can be exactly copied if the design isn't registered and protected.

Patents: Patents are aimed at things you invent. This is an extensive scope and can range from gadgets to medication and cosmetics. Patents aren't foolproof as competitors could recreate your invention but include minor design differences to avoid patent infringement. Here is an example in the field of cosmetics; your competitors could be producing the same kinds of products as you, but you can protect your best-selling creations by patenting them, preventing competitors from copying your exact formula.

When and How to Protect Intellectual Property

While copyright is automatically applied to intellectual property the moment it's created, it's not a bulletproof cover for your potential interests regarding the work. Ask yourself these questions in order to decide when to pursue legal protection, and help you which option to choose:

- "Can this product, service, or brand be launched for financial gain without infringing on anyone else's property rights?"
- If the answer is "yes" to the question above, then ask, "What part of the service, product, or brand can be protected?"
- Once you've decided what can be protected, ask, "Which protection option is most valuable for protecting your intellectual property and rights?"

Intellectual Property Protection Tips

Securing your intellectual property should commence well before it has been legally protected. For example, you could have a stroke of genius, but before you execute your idea, it could be stolen and protected by another party, thereby preventing you from any legal recourse. Here are some tips for protecting your creations at the moment inspiration strikes:

1. **Document development of your work:** Digitally documenting your progress, discoveries, and

creation development provides a digital record and fingerprint, including dating. If someone leaks your ideas, having that digital fingerprint as proof can establish ownership of intellectual property.

2. **Control access:** Use strong access credentials to restrict access to your ideas and work and limit who has those details. If multiple people can access shared files, opt for individual credentials to track who accessed what and when.

3. **Implement non-disclosure agreements:** These agreements legally bind any party privy to your sensitive information to keep your trade secrets under wraps. Should information be leaked, the culprit can be held legally responsible for damages caused as a result.

4. **Use Digital Rights Management (DRM):** Digital Rights Management offers a layer of protection for intellectual property accessible to clients, users, or fans online. More about that in a moment.

Digital Rights Management

In our age of digital media, intellectual property rights face new and evolving challenges, especially when it comes to work published online. Digital rights management (DRM) seeks to mitigate these challenges and uphold the protection of work belonging to individuals and organizations. Copyright laws suffer the drawback of focusing on recourse after the fact when intellectual property has been appropriated. In addition, the potential mass exposure of copyrighted work to a vast audience makes pursuing legal action against every perpetrator challenging to near impossible. This is where DRM comes in, and here's how it works:

1. **Access limitations:** These help deter even the most die-hard content thieves. Access limitations can include:
2. How many times the content can be copied or printed
3. How long the content can be accessed for
4. The types or brands of devices that can access the content
5. The number of devices that can access the content
6. The types of applications or software permitted on the devices accessing the content
7. Sharing or copying the content, even through screenshots
8. **Distortion:** Content is distorted and rendered unreadable if someone manages to copy it.
9. **Access credentials:** Access to content is limited to users who have an internet connection that uses some type of authentication before the content is accessible.
10. **Performance limitations:** Restricting the performance of the content, such as applications or software, if it's suspected of being used illegally.
11. **Watermarking:** A visible mark of ownership on the work, especially digital work. This is typically used for visual intellectual property, such as photographs.

Suppose you visit a professional photographer's website or an image-purchasing website. In that case, you may notice a script or a logo placed strategically on the image that indicates who owns it and renders it unusable by anyone else.

WHAT'S NEXT?

Understanding the different facets of cybersecurity, including the ethics and compliance laws, is the first step toward improving your own cybersecurity. The two previous chapters have laid the foundation for the next phase in enhancing your security and privacy. With the understanding you've gained, you can now begin working on creating and implementing a cybersecurity strategy of your own. In the next section, several chapters will cover a thorough step-by-step guide to cybersecurity products, services, and practices to improve your personal protection. The guide goes beyond just setting up and using security infrastructure such as firewalls and login credentials; it also tackles cybersecurity hygiene practices surrounding how you handle your data, approach privacy protection, and navigate living in an information and technology-driven world more safely.

PART II

SECURING AND PROTECTING YOUR DIGITAL LIFE

4

YOUR STEP-BY-STEP GUIDE TO CYBERSECURITY

Cybersecurity can be daunting to novices interested in safeguarding themselves from the perils of living in a technologically driven age. Many people may turn to tech blogs for answers, only to be greeted with a myriad of tongue-twisting terms and ambiguous acronyms. Many supposedly consumer-friendly resources provide information which is presented in terms and acronyms which only specialists and computer-literate people will understand. After all, they're written by the technically minded, and the lingo-savvy professionals who not only inherently have a mental knack for understanding technology but also have years of experience in the cybersecurity realm.

Even a search for answers to a question such term as innocuous as "What is a firewall?" can deliver results such as the following like, "A firewall is a network security device that monitors incoming and outgoing network traffic and permits or blocks data packets based on a set of security rules." (What is a firewall?, n.d.) In the first sentence of the explanation, it's already assumed that the reader knows what data packets are. Further reading reveals an even more discombobulating description, such as, "Source address 172.18.1.1 is allowed to reach destination 172.18.2.1 over port 22." (What is a firewall?, n.d.).

Now, these examples are by no means intended to target a single resource or to vilify the very effort aimed at educating the general population about cybersecurity and technology. The examples were chosen to illustrate how confusing and intimidating even explanations specifically directed at consumer education can be. After reading one or even several articles on cybersecurity and individual mechanisms for securing your privacy and sensitive information, you can easily be left asking a very pertinent question:

"Can I teach myself cybersecurity?"

The answer to that question is a resounding "Yes!". That is the whole point of this book: to help you learn about cyber-security and how to implement it in a way that is easy to follow, understand, and to get started. It's time to strengthen your cybersecurity with the help of this step-by-step guide. Discover how to improve what you're already doing and how to employ more measures to increase your protection for your everyday use of information technology.

5

STEP 1: CYBERSECURITY RISK ASSESSMENT

The first step toward improving your cybersecurity is to perform a cybersecurity risk assessment. The cybersecurity questionnaire at the end of chapter one was meant to bring awareness to the bare basics of your current cybersecurity risk. Now, we'll dive deeper into your security and potential vulnerabilities to perform a full-scale assessment. This will give you the big picture of how secure or exposed you and your sensitive data are to attack and exploitation.

Identify Your Data

What personal data do you have?

Think about any and all information that is valuable to you, including the following (but not limited to them):

- Full names and surnames

- Date of birth
- Identity number, social security number, passport number
- Contact details such as personal and professional e-mails, all messenger applications, phone numbers, physical address, and more – any details pertaining to any form of contact anybody could use to get in touch with you
- Place of work, job title, job responsibilities
- Familial information (including the identity of your extended family and how they are related to you)
- Financial information: bank account details, credit cards, store cards, rewards cards/programs
- Accounts and subscriptions such as social media, forums, blogs, websites, magazines or newspapers, application accounts, software accounts
- Home and vehicle information such as vehicle details (including make, model, and registration); home ownership details such as deeds or rental agreements
- Medical information including the names of all medical professionals you see, any medical records you have, your medical history, any medications you take, and prescriptions
- Miscellaneous information such as any other personally identifying or sensitive information. This may include legal information such as correspondence with lawyers, divorce papers, inheritance documents, etc.

- Proxy information such as digital or hard copies of any information about your friends, family, or others that could be affected if you were to fall victim to a cyberattack. This information may include all of the above points and everyday details about people's lives and activities. It could be anywhere from notes you've made to messages or emails.

Important note: This step of the process will likely be long and tedious. At first, taking stock of all your personal information can seem daunting and overwhelming. Use each of the above examples to break the process down into manageable chunks, and carefully take stock of *all* of your sensitive personal information. Even if there is some information that is in a physical hard copy, include it in your inventory. This is because so much information is now going digital. Medical and legal records are already digital, and what you have as a hard copy right now may become digital in the future even if you are not aware of it.

How Is the Data Stored and Where?

Please take all the data you identified in the previous section and note how and where you store it. Remember to include usernames, passwords, account numbers, and everything.

Methods of storing the data may include:

- **Hard copies:** Physical paper documents like sticky notes, printed bank statements, receipts, photocopies of documents, details written down in your daily planner, etc.

- **Digital copies:** PDFs, Word documents, Excel spreadsheets, Google documents, digital copies on the cloud, digital sticky notes, etc.

Where you store the data may include:

- **Hard copies:** In plain sight, such as lying on your desk or in a drawer accessible to family, friends, or coworkers, a bank safety deposit box, a home safe, etc.
- **Digital copies:** Email, cloud, on a device accessible to friends, family, or coworkers, hard drives, USB, mobile devices like phones or tablets, etc.

How Are the Data Protected?

How data are protected can significantly impact your chance of risk, whether it's in hardcopy or digital format. Physical protection can sometimes be better than digital protection. Still, sometimes your information has to interact with the digital world, making digital security awareness vitally important. Protection methods may include:

- **Hard copies:** safes, bank deposit boxes, locked rooms, etc.
- **Digital copies:** password-protected documents, accounts, and files to access control on devices and networks, firewalls, VPNs, and more.

Important note: When assessing how your information is protected, consider the strength of your passwords, whether you have two-factor authentication, and what other cybersecurity measures you have in place already.

How Long Do You Keep the Data?

This may seem like a silly question at face value, but it's really not. You may keep your identity number and bank account number for years, or even for your entire life. However, it would be best to consider not keeping the same account access credentials for extended periods. You may also want to think about whether you really still need a hard copy of a bank statement lying around from a decade ago. Here are some questions to help you along:

- How long do you keep hard copies or digital copies of certain information such as bank statements, prescriptions, and more?
- How often do you change your passwords for apps, accounts, etc.?
- Are you holding onto any past copies of information that you can delete?
- How long do you keep emails or messages backed up?

Who's Got Access to Your Data?

This is a critical question to ask yourself, with extremely wide-reaching implications. Here are some pertinent questions:

Who has access to your personal and work devices? This is a tricky question. It encompasses access to your devices when they are unlocked, as well as who has the passcodes to unlock your devices. Leaving a device unlocked and unattended, even for a few minutes, poses a significant risk, as anyone who walks by could snoop and discover sensitive information. Furthermore, if anybody knows the password or pin to unlock any of your devices, those devices are inherently at risk of breach.

Who has access to your accounts? This has more to do with who has your account usernames and passwords than asking who may directly access your accounts. If your accounts and applications have protected access, somebody may not be able to get in even if they have the passcode to unlock a device. However, even if someone doesn't have the passcode to unlock a device but has your username and password for accounts and applications, they could easily access your information from an entirely different device.

Information Value Assessment

Now that you have identified all personal information you possess, it's time to determine the value of that information. Personal information is not all of equal value, and the theft or harvesting of some of it can have extremely significant repercussions for your personal and professional life. These questions will help you determine what impact the leaking or theft of the information would have on your life if you were to come under fire from a cyberattack. You will need to separately assess each piece of information you've previously identified in step one of this assessment. So, take your time and really think about it all.

- What financial or legal damage could be done to you, personally or professionally, if the information is either exposed or lost?
- How valuable would this information be to someone with criminal intent or to a competitor of yours? What could they do if they had this information?
- If you lost this information, could you recover it? This includes resetting passwords to accounts. If you can recover it, how long would that take?
- What are the potential legal or financial implications of not being able to access accounts, applications, or devices while you are recovering the data or accounts?
- What kind of reputational damage could someone do to you, personally and professionally, if they accessed this information?

Identify and Prioritize Your Assets

You probably have multiple devices, various accounts, and numerous applications that need to be protected through cybersecurity. Implementing a solid cybersecurity strategy is a process, and it takes time. To begin the process, you must identify and prioritize your data, and your technology, in order to secure it. Once you have a list from most to least important data, devices, and software or applications to be secured, you can continue with the step of the process.

- List your personal data in order of importance based on how much of an impact it would have on your life if these data were either compromised or lost.
- List how and where the above data are stored, used, or shared.
- List the software or applications you use in order of importance based on how much impact it would have on your life if they were compromised or access lost.
- List your tech devices in order of importance based on how much it would negatively impact your life if they were compromised or access lost.

Important note: Sometimes, images, video, and other forms of "memories" aren't necessarily considered when evaluating your significant personal data. However, while they may not be as crucial as other information, such as banking details, they have sentimental value. Consider including file archives in this section for that purpose.

Identify Your Threat Landscape

So far, you have identified your valuable information, and then identified both where and how you store it, and who has access to it, and then you have even listed it in order of priority of its protection. Evaluating and implementing cybersecurity is a tremendous job, and you're doing great so far! Now, it's time to identify what your potential threats are. In this section, we're going to look at which cyber attacks you are likely to face. This will help you develop a strategy to protect yourself against them. Here are some common threats to consider:

Natural disasters: Cybersecurity usually focuses on protecting users from the human criminal element, but what about natural threats? Devices are particularly susceptible to natural disasters. Think of dropping your phone in water, having your laptop stolen, or having devices such as hard drives destroyed in a fire or damaged irreparably by lightning. In terms of physical damage to hardware caused by natural disasters, it could be worth considering backing up all essential data on a remote server, like the cloud.

Human error: This is a big one. Prevalent cyber attacks employ social engineering to trick individuals into divulging sensitive information. This could happen via email, text, phone calls, or other means. Consider how trusting you are and how readily you may give up vital information because someone seems legitimate. For example, if someone phoned you claiming to be from your mobile service provider and stated a scammer was trying to access your account and needed your cooperation to stop the threat, what would you do? They could ask that you provide personal information including, but not limited to, your name, account number, address, and event one-time pins to gain access to your account. Just because they claimed to be legitimate, would you believe them or be suspicious and refuse to give them the information they requested? This scenario can also play out over email or text or even as a message from someone impersonating a trusted friend of yours. You could also be duped into clicking on a malicious link via text, online, email, or social media. Human error is a massive factor in the success of social engineering attacks.

System failure: This comes down to the quality of your hardware and software and the level of support offered by the manufacturer. Using poor-quality hardware and software leaves you vulnerable to failure. However, even quality technology is only as good as the level of customer support you can get if it fails. What is the quality of your hardware and software, and what kind of support are you afforded. For example, free software can be very tempting, but it usually doesn't offer the same level of protection or support as paid-for versions.

Malicious threats: These threats include a wide variety of potential sources, including:

- People you know who have access to your information or to where it's stored
- Hackers and cybercriminals employ a variety of attack methods
- Competitors
- Third parties

Tip: Revisit the most common cyberattacks covered in chapter one to familiarize yourself with the most popular forms of attack and use those to help identify potential vulnerabilities.

Here are some common forms of malicious threats:

- **Unauthorized access:** This can come from hackers, malware, or even people you know accessing your information or accounts without permission.
- **Data leaks:** Anybody can leak data, including yourself. If you share sensitive information with someone else over an unsecured network, for instance, it could be intercepted by a cybercriminal. Other sources of data leaks include the companies, applications, and organizations you have accounts with who have and keep your personal information.
- **Information misuse:** These kinds of threats are usually from those you trust, such as friends, family, and others who know or have access to your crucial information. You need to identify who has access to what, and also identify who knows what, in order to determine whether you are at risk of your information being misused without your permission.

Assess Threat Likelihood

Now that you have identified potential threats, it's time to assess the likelihood and possible impact if that threat were to happen. This is commonly referred to, in the world of business, as performing a risk analysis. Although it is prudent to consider previous threats you've experienced, those historic threats shouldn't be your primary focus.

Look at each of the potential threats you have identified and determine the following:

1. What is the likelihood of such a cybersecurity breach happening or being successful? You can use a scale of 1-10 and rate the likelihood (with 1 being least likely of success). You may be tight-lipped about your passwords and never give them out to anyone, but use old equipment that already falters from time to time. In this scenario, you're less likely to fall victim to someone gaining unauthorized access to your information. Still, your risk of a system failure is relatively high.
2. What would the impact be if that form of cybersecurity breach occurred? Think about the potential reputational, financial, and operational consequences (operational referring to your ability to work or perform daily tasks).

Determine Your Cybersecurity Options

Having compiled a great deal of information by this point in your risk assessment, you're now finally at the point where you can use it to improve your security. Here are the next three steps to take:

- Prioritize potential threats based on your risk analysis. You'll need to address those with the highest likelihood and the greatest negative impact first and work your way down the list to threats of least concern.
- For each threat, there will be cybersecurity controls you can utilize to decrease your risk of attempted attacks being successful. Determine what security tools and protocols you can implement to lower your risk.
- Take your time to research your options for each tool or protocol. This will involve weighing up different services, brands, costs, and reviews. Once you've chosen your tools, you can start implementing them. (Some of these will be explained and discussed in the next section of the book).

WHAT'S NEXT?

That cybersecurity risk assessment was a lot of work. Well done! By completing the assessment, you have set a solid foundation for creating your cybersecurity strategy. You are now aware of all the sensitive and potentially valuable information you possess, and you have an idea of what level of security you're currently employing. If you're somewhat shocked by how much information you should be protecting and how vulnerable that information currently potentially is, don't worry! You are about to start discovering what the security basics are, and from there, you can start implementing them to strengthen your protection and privacy. In fact, simply learning about cybersecurity is already reducing your risk since those most at risk of cyber attacks are those who don't know much about it. In the next step, we'll discuss the basics of securing your devices and networks. The most crucial cybersecurity "must-haves" will be explained, from firewalls and antimalware to virtual private networks and practical tips for device and network protection best practices.

6

STEP 2: SECURE YOUR DEVICES
AND NETWORKS

his guide has been divided into logical steps for
creating and implementing a cybersecurity strategy to
be used easily and effectively by everyday users. After
performing an in-depth security risk assessment, figuring
out how to protect your information and which security
measures to implement can seem overwhelming. That's
okay. Take a step back, maybe even take a few days' break,
and then come back to the second step. The process has been
broken down into manageable steps, with each step
addressing a particular area of cybersecurity as opposed to
trying to explain everything at once. Step 2 focuses on
securing your devices and networks, such as computers,
tablets, smartphones, modems, routers, and Wi-Fi. This step
may contain overlapping information or suggestions which
are covered in a later step. If that's the case, it'll be indicated.
Everything in this step can be actioned immediately to

instantly improve your security. You can always revisit measures you have already put in place later down the line to increase their efficacy once you've learned even more.

FIREWALLS

Simply put, a firewall is a network security measure that blocks unauthorized or untrusted access to your network. Now, before the ins and outs of firewalls are discussed in more detail, it is worth explaining what is meant by a 'network', as it is vital to understanding the importance of firewalls. A network refers to how various pieces of technology are linked to perform different tasks, such as sharing files. Anything that allows you to connect one device to another or to connect a device to the internet can be considered a network, from Wi-Fi to Bluetooth, to wired networking through hardware cables.

A firewall can be likened to perimeter fencing and controlled gate access around a property. The fence keeps trespassers out, and controlled gate access allows only trusted people to enter the property while turning away unwanted visitors. This is precisely what a firewall does. It monitors incoming and outgoing traffic over any network your device is connected to and stops untrusted or potentially harmful traffic reaching your device or blocks unauthorized outgoing traffic from leaving.

Hardware Vs. Software

There are two predominant forms of firewalls: hardware and

software. Hardware firewalls are physical units plugged in between your computer and the network. In contrast, software firewalls are applications that run from within your device. They both perform the same job, but they go about it slightly differently.

Hardware Firewalls

- A single firewall unit can protect multiple devices simultaneously.
- Suppose a single unit is employed to safeguard multiple devices. In that case, it implies that if the firewall is compromised, all network parts are simultaneously compromised.
- A single update to the unit automatically upgrades protection across all network devices at once.
- Firewall configuration applies to the entire network as the configuration is only done for the firewall unit.
- Hardware units have their own operating system, and so they don't put a strain on your device's processing power or memory.
- The firewall protection isn't susceptible to fluctuation based on a device's processing or memory capabilities, and so offers constant protection.
- Hardware units are stationary, and devices must be in the same location as the unit to be protected.

Software Firewalls

- The firewall application has to be installed on each network device separately.
- Suppose one device's firewall application is compromised. In that case, the rest of the network is still protected by individual firewalls on each device.
- Updates have to be done on each device's firewall application separately.
- Each device's firewall application settings have to be configured separately.
- Firewall applications don't have their own operating systems. Instead, they tap into your device's processing and memory, potentially draining speed and taking up digital space, which could affect your user experience.
- The protection is vulnerable to fluctuation if the device's memory or processing is affected.
- Software firewalls protect devices that are not in the same location, making them ideal for remote or mobile interaction between employees.

Types of Firewalls

Firewalls can be classified according to their primary purpose and the tasks they perform while doing their job to uphold your network security. Here are the types of firewalls you need to know about and how they work:

Packet filtering: To understand how packet filtering firewalls work, the term 'packet' needs to be explained. A packet is one of the building blocks of data. Irrespective of the type of data sent, such as text, audio, video, or images, the data are broken down into smaller packets, like puzzle pieces. The packets are sent from the source to the destination, where the receiving device reassembles them into one piece, like building the puzzle to render the whole picture. Data are broken down into packets to maximize network usage. If you were to send data as a long, continuous chain of bits, you'd be hogging the network path, thus preventing other users from accessing the path until you're done. By sending individual packets, multiple users can use the same network simultaneously. The packets can also travel from the source to the destination using different network paths.

A packet-filtering firewall monitors the packets being sent to and from your network. How the firewall determines whether to block packets is defined by your configuration settings. It will block packets from being received or sent based on where they're coming from, where they're going, application protocols, and other parameters. This kind of firewall is also known as a stateless firewall.

Stateful firewall: A stateful firewall doesn't just analyze data sent over a network connection. It monitors and collects information about every connection, using this information to create a list of characteristics that indicate safe connections. When the user tries to make a connection, the firewall analyzes the characteristics of the requested connection. If the analysis suggests the connection has safe qualities, it will allow the connection to happen. If not, the firewall will get rid of the data packets before they can be sent or received. There are three aspects to how a stateful firewall works:

- **Transmission Control Protocol (TCP):** TCP is a standard of communication that allows applications and devices to send and receive data through a network. It defines how connections are created and maintained for the exchange of data. The TCP protocol breaks data into packets, sending them from the source to the destination and reassembling them again once they've been received. Stateful firewalls use a protocol to their advantage through the TCP three-way handshake and stateful packet inspection.
- **Stateful packet inspection:** The contents of data packets are inspected and compared to data packets that have previously been sent or received. The information the firewall can glean from examining the packets also provides insight about the sender, receiver, packet sequencing, and what's in the packet. All of this information is used to detect any potential threats.
- **Three-way handshake:** TCP utilizes a three-way handshake to establish a connection between users over a network. Both parties synchronize to create the connection and then acknowledge each other. While this handshake is being established, a stateful

firewall will examine the information being exchanged from both sides of the connection to identify whether the connection has the qualities to be deemed safe and whether the data being transferred poses a potential threat. The connection and data packets can then be allowed or discarded.

Stateful firewalls analyze data packets using more information than stateless firewalls, making them a better choice for small businesses and enterprises.

Proxy firewall: You've probably heard the phrase "by proxy" before, usually when someone or something is represented by another. The word 'proxy' means someone or something has the authority to act on behalf of a client. Proxy firewalls are also sometimes called gateway firewalls. They act as a gateway for communication between users on your network and other networks via the internet. They don't monitor traffic between users on your internal network; their purpose is to monitor and control communication between your network users through the internet to other networks. Proxy firewalls prevent users or applications from sending or receiving malicious network connection requests over the internet through a browser interface. Proxy firewalls are also sometimes called application-level gateways.

Circuit-level gateway: Like packet-filtering firewalls, circuit-level gateways are simple protection systems. Their job is to check and monitor the connection between networks through the TCP handshake. They're not concerned with inspecting the contents of data packets. Their other job is to act as a virtual connection between the user's secure network and other networks, obscuring the user's IP address from other networks.

Next-generation firewall (NGFW): NGFWs do everything stateful firewalls do and more. They take your firewall protection to the next level by offering the same protection as their stateful cousins, as well as:

- Intrusion prevention
- Intrusion detection
- Advanced malware detection
- Application awareness to control network connections on the application level, blocking apps presenting a potential threat
- Threat intelligence, allowing up-to-date protection by accessing the most recent threat identification information
- Virtual private network awareness to identify encrypted virtual private networks and allow connections and traffic

Cloud service firewalls: Cloud services are on the rise as an online option for backing up and storing data of all sorts, from images to documents. Keeping data in a readily accessible online space that isn't subject to the same vulnerabilities as physical storage devices, such as hardware malfunction or physical damage, is convenient and appealing. For example, suppose you lose your physical passport while traveling. In that case, you can access a digital copy from the cloud without the inconvenience of having a hard copy sent to you. However, this increasingly popular form of online backup and storage poses its own security challenges. Being based in the online realm, physical access restrictions don't apply, and the cloud is potentially susceptible to the same kinds of attacks as other online accounts, applications, and platforms.

One solution to possible pitfalls of cloud service security is to use a cloud firewall. These are sometimes referred to as firewalls-as-a-service or FWaaS. These digital firewalls act in the same manner as a regular hardware or network firewall. They form a barrier between the internet, where the cloud is hosted, and your personal cloud account. The firewall is offered "as a service" provided by a third-party provider. Unfortunately, these services are subject to the same concerns as other third-party services, such as provider integrity and their own security levels. You can partially negate these concerns by thoroughly researching your options and making your decision based on a provider's reputation, features, and security level. Choosing a reputable provider usually equals better protection, functionality, and system integrity.

What are the benefits of a cloud firewall or FWaaS?

- It's convenient; a third-party provider handles all your updates.

- You can, with one service, protect multiple cloud accounts.
- It easily integrates with the cloud service you are using.
- It doesn't require you to have any additional hardware devices to gain the protection.
- Its service can easily be scaled up to handle increased traffic.
- It guards against various online malicious traffic, including harmful automated bot activity and malware.
- It can even stop outgoing traffic containing sensitive data.

Smartphone on-device firewalls: Since firewalls can be software or hardware, it stands to reason that you can employ the software version on your mobile devices, such as smartphones and tablets. These firewalls offer you an additional layer of protection. Interestingly, some smartphones have built-in firewalls, such as various iPhone models. Even if some devices are said to have this nifty feature, always check to confirm it has a built-in firewall and that it's activated. It is not wise to just assume the firewall is built in.

Firewall Limitations

A firewall is the first line of defense for any information technology user. It's the first step toward securing your device or network from a cyberattack. However, a firewall is not infallible and should be used with other security measures, including stringent cyber hygiene. Firewall protection has limitations:

- It can't protect you from a variety of social engineering attacks.
- It may not fully protect you from vulnerabilities that arise with authorized communications over trusted connections and applications.
- It can be susceptible to configuration vulnerabilities. They can only safeguard you using the rules given to them by whoever configures the settings.
- It can't protect your data if communication doesn't pass through the firewall. Protection is not offered by a firewall for telephone calls or text messages, for example.
- It can't protect secure applications against Trojan horse malware or tunneling attacks.

ANTI-X SOFTWARE

Anti-X software comes in various forms, including antivirus, antimalware, antispyware, and antiransomware. It can be difficult to know what they all do, and which one to use.

Let's start off by revisiting what malware is. It's any malicious software that can infect your device, system, or network. As such, viruses are considered malware. Malware is an umbrella term for all sorts of different malicious software, and there are two main malicious software protection options; antivirus and antimalware. It is worth discussing the difference between the two.

As the name implies, antivirus programs were initially designed to specifically protect against computer viruses. However, malicious software has evolved beyond being merely computer viruses and now includes many more forms of cyberattack. Antivirus programs have evolved alongside the development of different types of malware. They can now address both viruses and classic types of malware. The shortcoming of this software is that it doesn't handle newer or lesser-known types of malware, and that's where malware protection comes in.

Antimalware programs weren't developed to replace traditional antivirus software. Instead, they seek to complement it to enhance your cybersecurity further. Antivirus software offers a basic defense against more conventional viruses and malicious attacks. Antimalware programs aim to strengthen your security by including a broader spectrum of malicious software and focusing on more elaborate attacks.

As for which one you should choose, the answer is both. Having an antivirus program is the first step in your digital protection, but because it's not comprehensive, adding malware to your arsenal creates multi-layer protection, which increases what you're protected against. Answering the question of which antivirus and antimalware programs to choose, on the other hand, is trickier. Ultimately, it comes down to personal preference and budget, but here's what to look for in both programs:

Antivirus Features

- Virus scans
- Automatic updates
- Blocking of malicious script files
- Heuristic analysis (a way to identify previously known versions as well as new virus variants)
- Compilation of a malware database
- Removal of malware (various free versions of antivirus programs only·block malware from running but don't remove them)
- Protection against ransomware

Antimalware Features

- Scanning, detection, and removal of malware
- Automatic updates
- Anti-phishing
- Anti-exploitation kit protection
- Protection against malware distribution through websites
- Online banking protection
- Sandboxing (creating a safe environment to test potential threats to determine their safety)
- Second-generation malware protection
- Specialized malware protection database
- Traffic filtering (protection against attack from infected servers)

INTRUSION DETECTION AND PREVENTION SYSTEMS

The name says it all. A system for detecting and preventing intrusion. The IDPS observes traffic or activity on a device or network in order to identify potential malicious activity, to prevent malicious attacks, and to alert the system administrator of the possible intrusion. Some people consider firewalls and anti-x software to be types of IDPS, especially with modern renditions that alert the user to potential threats. The problem with this conflation is that the configuration and capabilities of these mechanisms may be limited to simply detecting and blocking attempted attacks without notifying the user or system administrator. Additionally, the sophistication of your firewall and anti-x software may not stop new developments in the ever-evolving landscape of cybercrime intrusions. For this reason, we'll classify IDPS on its own.

Types of Intrusion Detection and Prevention Systems

Depending on the needs of the user or system administrator, there are four main types of IDPS available:

Host-based (HIDPS): This system safeguards a single endpoint or device. A host-based IDPS performs the following functions:

- Collecting data from the device system
- Monitoring the activity on the networks the device is connected to

- Confirming if any unusual activity is happening on the device or networks it's connected to
- Alerting the user of any suspected suspicious activity
- Blocking the attempted attack

Network-based (NIDPS): Activity and traffic on a network as a whole is monitored. Individual device system data aren't collected. A NIDPS observes traffic within the network and uses two methods for detecting potentially malicious activity. It looks at packet metadata, what's in it, and monitors protocol activity. In order to root out possible intrusion attempts, activity and data are analyzed using a database of known attacks.

Wireless (WIDPS): A wireless network is monitored to detect unauthorized access and unusual network activity according to established networking protocols.

Network behavior analysis (NBA): An NBA seeks out behavioral patterns within the network, rather than analyzing network traffic according to protocols. It monitors the network for abnormal traffic flows that may result from policy violations, malware, and other kinds of cyber attacks.

Types of Detection and Prevention Methods

There are different methods of detecting intrusion attempts, and each type of IDPS will employ one or more of the following methods:

Signature-based: Different cyber attacks usually have an identifiable signature, like a fingerprint. A signature-based IDPS will use this signature from a known database to detect intrusion attempts. The drawback of this detection method is that it only protects against previously identified cyberattack signatures, not against unfamiliar attacks.

Anomaly-based: This method relies on monitoring behavioral patterns of devices, users, systems, applications, and networks. If any abnormal behavior is identified, it's flagged as a potential threat. This method offers better protection against evolving cyberattacks, but it can also produce a higher percentage of false positives or false alarms. Just because behavior deviates from the norm doesn't necessarily indicate an attack, but it's usually a good clue.

Protocol-based: The protocols used by a system, network, or host detect potential malicious activity by looking for deviations from the usual protocols.

Intrusion Detection vs. Intrusion Protection

An IPS is inherently an IDS as it needs to be able to detect the intrusion before it can prevent it, but an IDS doesn't necessarily prevent the attack. The IDS will alert the system administrator, but that's where its job ends. As such, you would think that an IPS is automatically the better option, but that isn't always the case, especially in dynamic environments. Dynamic environments are those where things are constantly changing. This may include alterations to device setups, systems, the kinds of data being handled, and what devices are connected to a network. Attempts at unauthorized access in such fast-changing environments that are continually in flux can be challenging to detect and prevent, making an IDS that can quickly adapt to this ever-changing environment invaluable.

An IPS is meant to not only detect but also respond to a suspected cyberattack according to a set of predetermined rules. The system administrator doesn't even have to be involved in containing the attack; the IPS does it automatically. Methods of preventing potential attacks include quarantining data files, ending processes, and stopping network traffic, among others. The problem posed by using an IPS is the risk of legitimate network activity, users, applications, processes, and more being blocked. It may react to and mitigate a potential threat faster due to automatic responsiveness, but it can cause a headache if false positives are a common occurrence, such as in anomaly-based systems.

FIREWALL VS. IDS VS. IPS

With so many baseline cybersecurity options available, you may wonder which one you need and whether you need more than one solution. The complexity and ever-changing nature of cybercrime make multi-layer protection a highly recommended approach. So, you'll likely want to employ different security measures simultaneously instead of relying on just one.

A firewall is your first line of defense, protecting your system by blocking any unauthorized or suspicious traffic. A firewall is unable to alert the system administrator of potential attacks and is unable to prevent attacks that may piggyback into your secure cyberspace on communication from a legitimate source.

An IDS lets you know when a suspected attack is detected, but it does nothing to block or prevent the possible attack. The responsibility for containing the attack falls onto another technology or a human system administrator. The advantage is that legitimate activity flagged as a false positive can be inspected and allowed to continue without disrupting interactions and potentially halting or slowing down workflow. Unfortunately, the time it takes for the system administrator to check and verify whether or not the suspicious activity is legitimate, and can spell disaster.

An IPS is designed to work hand-in-hand with your firewall and offer automatic responses to suspected attacks to quickly contain the threat. If an attack makes it past your firewall, the IPS will alert you to the possible threat and go to work to prevent it from being successful. When implemented in a dynamic environment where network and user behavior vary greatly, it can mistake legitimate behavior for suspicious activity, and then erroneously associate it with a possible threat.

Ultimately, a firewall is a cybersecurity necessity. Whether you opt for an IDS or an IPS depends on whether you want action taken against suspected malicious activity automatically, or prefer to be alerted to it and then have the system administrator decide what to do about it. However, just having these measures in place mustn't be where your cyber-security ends. Connecting to public networks and the internet is still a risky business, and you should consider further steps to protect your privacy and sensitive data, such as using a virtual private network as a secure connection portal to the rest of the world.

UPDATE SOFTWARE

Software, like most information technology, is constantly evolving and advancing, which means there are always new updates appearing. Updates are intended to offer users improvements to the functionality or fixes for existing problems. It can be tempting to ignore prompts to update your software, including applications, but there are a couple of vital reasons you should continually update when a new one is available.

Security

Software engineers are human, and as such, their work isn't going to be perfect. Sometimes, a software version can have security flaws at the time of its release. Updates often include patches to fix these flaws when they are detected. In addition to fixing existing flaws, cybercriminals are constantly seeking new ways to exploit software vulnerabilities, and from time to time, they manage to come up with new attacks. Updates also include new security measures to combat the constantly changing threat landscape and protect you from emerging threats.

Bugs

Software updates involve complex processes and changes to a previous version, and this often results in bugs and issues. Try as they might, it's usually impossible for developers to identify and fix every bug before releasing an update. User feedback, which reports and explains the bug or issue, is valuable to help developers track down and resolve any remaining bugs that were overlooked before releasing the previous update. Those improvements can then be applied in the new update.

Performance

Updates don't just fix security issues and bugs. They also address the software's performance on your device. If you've ever resisted installing updates for an extended period, you might have noticed your device or a particular program beginning to slow down and experience performance issues. Regularly updating your software will avoid performance taking a knock by introducing improvements to keep things running smoothly.

New Features

The general expectation of updates is to add new features or enhance existing ones. This is only a tiny part of the purpose of updates, and they may not necessarily increase your cybersecurity, but as software updates are useful for the smooth running of your system in general, it can be seen as a welcome bonus that updates allow you to improve current features and add new ones will likely make your user experience more enjoyable.

Automatic Updates

Software updates can be performed manually, or you can enable automatic updates. Enabling automatic updates can be highly convenient. You will not have to regularly check if updates are available, nor will you have to schedule time to install them if they are; the software will do it all for you. This is useful if you have a busy schedule or if you tend to forget to manually update things. However, there are potential drawbacks.

The device must have a secure and stable Wi-Fi connection to check for and download updates, and the download itself will use data. If you are running low or are on a tight data budget, an automatic update can unexpectedly chew up what you have. Updates, especially bigger ones, can also take some time to install once downloaded, which can be inconvenient if you need to use your device during the installation period.

Your device must have enough storage space to accommodate the update, and you should make sure your information is backed up or saved before the update is installed. Enabling automatic updates means your device can download, install, and restart, and you may lose any unsaved work or information in the process.

Tip: Ensure your update settings conform to your preferences, including when to download and install them. Some settings will allow notification of available updates but request permission to download and install them. Other settings necessitate the connection of your device to a power source before downloading and installing updates to prevent the battery from being drained. Always take care when selecting update settings.

Modems and Routers

Modems and routers are often overlooked when it comes to software updates as they tend to sit stationary somewhere, usually out of view, and you don't directly interact with them. Ensure the software on these network devices is regularly updated, and the manufacturer still supports that device, especially for older models. If the model is no longer supported with continued updates, it's time to invest in a new device that will receive vital security updates.

Tip: Not all network device manufacturers offer security updates, especially those providing cheaper, lower-quality products. Avoid opting for modems and routers from manufacturers who do not provide regular updates.

SECURE WI-FI NETWORKS

Regarding Wi-Fi networks, it's vital to understand the difference between modems and routers. If you're not familiar with the terms, they may seem confusing. Simply put, they perform different jobs:

- A modem facilitates internet connection.
- A router facilitates the connection of your devices to

the internet connection provided by the modem. In hard-wired systems, a router connects to the modem to do that.

Years ago, both a modem and a router were needed in order to bring an internet connection to a home or workspace and then to link devices to that internet connection. However, as technology has evolved, the option to amalgamate modem and router functionality into a single device has become available. Think of this 2-in-1 merger as the connectivity equivalent of new-generation firewalls. Instead of having to invest in and maintain two separate network devices, you can now get the functionality of both in a single device. Irrespective of whether you use a single, all-in-one device or two different devices, you need to secure your Wi-Fi connection.

To protect your Wi-Fi network:

- Immediately change the default password and use strong login credentials to increase security.
- Restrict how many devices can connect to your Wi-Fi network at any one time to prevent unauthorized access when all authorized devices are connected.
- Enable encryption on your router or modem-router combo device.
- Use a virtual private network.

VIRTUAL PRIVATE NETWORKS

Have you ever used a virtual private network (VPN) before? VPNs are becoming increasingly popular around the world. Here are a few statistics to reflect their increasing usage:

- 66% of U.S. cyber users have used a VPN at some point.
- 33% of all internet access is done via a VPN.
- 72% of users on laptops or desktops use a VPN.
- 69% of mobile device users employ a VPN.
- 66% of VPN users use them to protect personal data.
- 50% of VPN users operate it on public Wi-Fi.
- 80% of VPN users use them for increased cybersecurity.

(Crail, 2023)

As you can see, VPN usage is becoming commonplace. If you still need to get started with using a VPN, let's dive into what it is and why you need to consider it as part of your cybersecurity arsenal.

What Is a VPN?

A VPN is a medium for creating a secure connection to a network, especially to vulnerable networks like public Wi-Fi. It's designed to offer users protection by encrypting the online traffic being sent and received by the user's device. It also protects and retains online privacy by hiding the user's identity, such as their location, or IP address. A VPN will also hide a user's online activity, including browsing history, which could otherwise be tracked by websites and other entities.

A VPN offers security and anonymity by routing your connection to the internet through the VPN host's remote server. The server is configured to act as the source of your online interaction, so your activity and data being sent and received is obscured from the view of your internet service provider (ISP) and from the view of any other third parties. However, it's more complicated because simply rerouting your traffic through the host server could continue to pose a security risk. A VPN further protects your data by scrambling it, so it is unintelligible. So, even if your information was illegally accessed it would be useless.

The benefits of using a VPN include:

- **Hiding your location:** VPN servers act like proxies. The server is located elsewhere, making your actual location hard, if not impossible, to determine.
- **Content access:** Some regional content is only accessible to users in specific locations. Employing a VPN server located in a different part of the world allows you to both shield your actual location as well as appear to change your location so that regional content is accessible, even though you're not in the region you seem to be.
- **Encryption:** Your data are converted into code that requires an encryption key to render it readable.

Without the encryption key, even if someone did manage to get hold of your data, they wouldn't be able to read it.

- **Data transfer:** A VPN is a secure way to connect to private servers where sensitive information may be stored. This secure connection reduces both the risk of sensitive information being accessed and of the risk of the information being leaked by unauthorized parties.

Using a VPN can significantly boost your online security, but it's not foolproof. As with any other form of hardware or software technology, it can come under cyberattack. How do you further secure your connection to bolster your protection from potential VPN vulnerabilities? The answer is multi-factor authentication, and this will be discussed later in the book.

AVOID USING PUBLIC WI-FI

Public Wi-Fi networks are often unsecured, which opens the door for cybercriminals to intercept your communications or to pursue other avenues of attack. Avoid using these threat-laden connections whenever possible. Instead, consider opting for a personal hotspot for your mobile phone or setting your phone up as a hotspot for your other gadgets such as your laptops and tablets. Do follow the protocols for securing access to your hotspot by using strong login credentials.

CONTROL ACCESS TO DEVICES AND NETWORKS

The more people with access to a device or network, the higher the risk of a security breach. It's vital to restrict access to as few users as possible and to control who has access. Here are four effective ways:

Avoid leaving devices unattended: This applies to devices like computers and smartphones, and to network devices like modems and routers. It's not always possible to keep an eye on all your devices all the time. However, whenever possible, avoid leaving mobile devices such as laptops, smartphones, and the like unattended where anybody could gain physical access to them.

Control physical access: Something simple like handing your unlocked phone over to a friend to look at a photo or read an article can lead to disaster, even unintentionally. Be careful of whom you allow physical access to your devices, including network devices. If necessary, lock the room the devices are in or lock them away in a cupboard to prevent anyone besides the keyholder from accessing them.

Use login credentials: All devices and networks should be access-controlled through login credentials, such as a username and password. If you have a shared device, such as a family laptop or computer, ensure each person who needs to use it has a separate user login to keep your information protected.

Enable automatic logout: Devices such as laptops, tablets, and mobile phones should be set to automatically log you out and lock after a certain period of inactivity. It's best to always log out or lock your devices when you aren't actively using them, but in today's busy life, it's easy to forget. Enabling automatic logout and locking adds a measure of protection against unauthorized access if you do forget to do it.

CHECK YOUR PRIVACY SETTINGS

This can be done on any device that supports applications or software with privacy controls, not just smartphones. Many apps offer users the option to customize their privacy settings to control what kind of information and how much is collected or shared. Check and consciously tailor privacy settings across every app or program you use, including browsers, streaming services, games, cloud services, and more. Your vigilance shouldn't stop there, though. It's worthwhile to regularly audit privacy settings for each app, such as after an update, to ensure no settings have changed.

STOP AUTOMATIC UPLOADS

Various applications across different devices offer the option to automatically back up your information to cloud services or remote servers. While this may seem like the height of convenience, it could also be highly unsafe. Regularly backing up your data should form part of your cybersecurity framework (more will be mentioned on this topic later in the guide), but all backups should be done entirely within your control and only to a location with restricted access. Cloud services and remote servers offered by applications may not be the most secure places to store your information. Prevent your data from escaping your complete control by disabling automatic uploads.

SET UP REMOTE LOCATION FEATURES AND REMOTE WIPING

Mobile devices, such as laptops, tablets, and smartphones, are at risk of being stolen or lost. There are applications available that will help you use other devices to locate your lost or stolen gadgets. Even if you can locate your devices, your information could still be at risk. Back up your remote location options with remote device wiping. These applications or features will allow you to wipe sensitive information from the device if it does fall into the wrong hands, minimizing both the damage and the other repercussions from loss or theft.

CHANGE DEFAULT PASSWORDS IMMEDIATELY

The best practice for dealing with your passwords will be covered later in the guide to help you create strong login credentials. However, many devices, such as modems and routers, have default passwords. When setting up any device that has an initial default password, change it immediately.

Switching to a more secure, personalized password strengthens your login credentials to prevent unauthorized access.

CHECK PUSH NOTIFICATION SETTINGS

Those notifications that pop up on your smartphone's home screen from applications are called 'push notifications'. They're generally convenient for keeping you up to date with information and updates from apps without much effort on your part unless, of course, you have many apps on your phone. However, some of these pop-up notifications could accidentally leak sensitive information. It is useful to look at each application, find out what it's used for, what kind of information it pops up on your screen, and decide whether you really need to be notified about it. Push notifications can often be previewed on your lock screen, meaning that someone doesn't have to be looking over your shoulder to get a peek at what the notification says or is about. Avoid accidentally leaving yourself vulnerable by curating your push notification settings. Here, you can disable notifications that may make personal information visible, and you can choose whether notifications should be brief or more detailed, for example.

SWITCH OFF BLUETOOTH

Bluetooth pairing with other devices usually involves a request sent from the device that wants to connect to yours, and you then grant or deny permission. Despite this, cyber-criminals can sometimes get around this request and grant or deny a process when attempting an attack. However, they can only try an attack if your Bluetooth is switched on. If it's not, there's no way to exploit your Bluetooth. Always keep your Bluetooth switched off when you're not actively using it to safeguard against the function being exploited to your detriment.

COVER YOUR WEBCAM

Most devices these days have a webcam. They allow face-to-face interactions online, such as during remote meetings or just catching up with friends or family over a video call. They're also helpful for recording and creating online content. Webcams do, unfortunately, have a downside. They can be used to eavesdrop or even spy on your conversations or whatever else you are doing. Simply pointing a webcam at a blank wall or at the ceiling doesn't guarantee your privacy since criminals may be listening in on conversations even if they can't actually see what you're up to. To avoid prying eyes and ears from invading your privacy, cover built-in laptop cams or switch off external webcams when you're not using them. Remember to disable built-in microphones, and switch off external ones to prevent others from eavesdropping on your conversations.

WHAT'S NEXT?

You have taken the first step toward increasing your cyber-security. You can now make a knowledgeable decision about various measures which can be put in place to protect your devices and networks. If you're still wondering about two-factor authentication for a VPN, then read on, because that is in the next step. Coming up is a guide to securing your accounts and information, and it will focus on practical measures for maximizing your cybersecurity for account or application logins and backing up your data to ensure you don't take a knock if the original copies are somehow lost or damaged. It's worth remembering that cybersecurity measures overlap in different areas. It may be worth your while to implement as many of the measures in the first step as you are able, before moving on to the next step. You can always revisit a measure if you learn something new that can improve your information's security.

7

STEP 3: SECURE YOUR ACCOUNTS AND INFORMATION

Securing your online accounts and your digital data will be the next steps to take to improve your cybersecurity. Increasing control of account access and improving data storage security will entail measures and principles that overlap with measures described in the previous step (which explained how to secure devices). These measures will make online browsing and social media use safer as you take further steps. It's worth revisiting the practices and measures you put in place in step 1 and apply what you have learned to make them more secure. In this step, we'll be looking at passwords, email protection, multifactor authentication, and data storage.

PASSWORDS

Passwords and PINs are the go-to forms of access authorization in cybersecurity. They're used almost everywhere, from logging into devices and accounts to connecting to networks. This makes addressing your password security strength your first port of call when securing your information. Creating a strong password is essential to thwart attempted security breaches. The problem is many people don't realize how weak their passwords are or what to avoid when creating a password. This has led many apps and account services to prompt people to use stronger passwords by requiring different letters, numbers, and symbols. This can be frustrating, particularly if you are prone to forgetting your password, but it's crucial to create the most secure passwords you can, else cybercriminals can simply use standard password-cracking software to access your devices, data, and networks. Here are some key aspects to think about in order to create stronger, more secure passwords:

Length: The shorter a password is, the easier it is to guess or crack. Opt for passwords of 8-16 characters long.

Complexity: Complex passwords are more challenging obstacles for cybercriminals. Be sure to use as many different types of characters as possible, including upper- and lower-case letters, numbers, and special characters. To make your passwords complex but easier to remember, try these tips:

- Avoid using a single word password preceded or followed by a single number, such as "Password2". It's all too easy for hackers to guess your password using either commonly used words or even a dictionary.
- Opt for a phrase or a sentence. This can increase complexity while simultaneously making it easier to remember. For example: "ButterTheKingSaidAnd-BouncedOutOfBed".

Type of information: Avoid using certain types of information in your passwords. Cybercriminals can easily make use of your personal information if it is readily available to others, so using personally identifiable information is a bad idea. This includes:

- Any information available on social media, websites, and other online spaces
- Names of friends and family members, including spouses, children, and extended family
- Names of pets
- Nicknames
- Car make and model
- Addresses
- Birthdates
- Old or current schools
- Old or current towns
- Favorite things such as animals, locations, colors, sports, and hobbies

- Social security numbers, passport numbers, and identity numbers
- Old or current phone numbers

Creating a strong password is only the first step in improving your password protection. Even if you come up with what seems like a pretty bulletproof password, you should consider the following password hygiene practices to strengthen your cybersecurity even further:

Vary passwords: One of the biggest mistakes you can make is using the same password for multiple logins. You may have many different logins, from your Wi-Fi to email, social media, and so on. It might seem easier to use one password for multiple logins to make it easier to remember your passwords. The problem is, if someone guesses one password, they're likely to try it on multiple accounts or devices just on the off-chance you've used the same password. If you have used one password for many devices and logins, cybercriminals who have guessed a password for one account or log-in of yours will then have access to a broad spectrum of sensitive information. Use a different password for each login.

Change them regularly: There's some debate about this one. Some say you should change your passwords every so often to keep cybercriminals guessing. In contrast, others say it's not really necessary. Those who advocate regular password changes may be onto something, though. The longer you have the same password, the easier it could become for someone to discover it. You may also be at a higher risk of accidentally revealing information that could be used to guess the password. However, whether you switch up your passwords regularly or not, you should definitely change them in the case of a life-changing event, such as a breakup or divorce, especially if you have shared any passwords with your partner.

Keep them secret: It can be tempting to share some passwords with people you feel you can trust, such as a sibling, best friend, parent, or significant other. It can even seem convenient. Resist temptation and avoid convenience for the sake of your security. Never reveal your password to anyone, no matter how much you feel you can trust them. It allows them access to your information and creates an additional security vulnerability, even if the people you have shared your passwords with have no malicious intent.

Avoid storing them: With potentially dozens of logins, you may be tempted to document and store your passwords somewhere. Avoid doing this. All it takes to compromise your sensitive information and login details is for someone to find where you've written them down or access where you're storing them. If you have a hard time remembering passwords and need to have them saved somewhere, consider using a secure password manager.

Use auto-lock: Some accounts or logins offer the option to lock you out of the account or device if the incorrect password is inserted multiple times. If any of your logins provide this function, enable it. If someone is trying to sneak their way into your account or device, they will only have a handful of attempts before they are barred from doing so. You will be notified your account is locked and have to follow the proper channels to get it unlocked again, but at least your information was protected.

Never save passwords: Various browsers offer the option to save your passwords for auto-login the next time you visit a site or application. Always decline this option or disable it altogether. It may be convenient for you, but if anyone gains access to your device, they can automatically log into the accounts, websites, or applications the passwords are saved for. Be especially vigilant when using shared household or public devices such as library computers.

MULTIFACTOR AUTHENTICATION

As the name implies, multifactor authentication (MFA) is a multi-faceted method of authenticating a user's identity. MFA can be used in many areas of cybersecurity, from accessing a VPN to accessing online accounts such as emails and applications. MFA requires a user to supply more than just a username and password before they are granted access. This dramatically increases your security because a hacker needs more information, making an attack less likely to succeed.

Three primary forms of MFA could be requested in addition to a username:

Knowledge: A user may be asked to authenticate themselves by providing additional information they know, such as:

- Personal security question answers
- Password
- One-time PIN

Possession: A user confirms authentication by using something they have in their possession or have access to, such as:

- A One-time PIN sent to the user's smartphone or email address
- physical key, such as an access badge, smart card, or USB
- Program certificates or tokens

Inherence: A user is asked for authentication using biometrics or unique physical characteristics, such as:

- Facial recognition
- Fingerprints
- Retina or iris scanning
- Voice recognition

Let's talk about using biometrics as part of MFA as it's becoming more popular. Even smartphones are bringing in biometric security features such as fingerprint scanners. This form of authentication is becoming more widely used, and although it is paving the way for future data security, it has potential challenges. For example, injury to a user's finger, such as a burn or abrasion, can temporarily or even permanently damage the fingerprint. A common cold could alter a user's voice, making it unrecognizable. Even something as simple as a change of camera angle or the wearing of colored contact lenses could interfere with facial recognition. So, it's worth considering which biometrics should be used, and when, before implementing these measures as part of your security.

EMAIL

Email is one of the most common forms of online communication. It's used by almost everybody, from individuals to businesses. It's also simple yet versatile, allowing various communication mediums to be sent and received, including text, images, video, and a wide assortment of other attachment files. Top all of that off with the option to implement filing systems and autoresponders when you're busy or on vacation. This makes email an attractive avenue of attack for cybercriminals as it is a potential treasure trove for them.

Secure Email Services

One solution is to send and receive secure email. Encryption is employed in two ways to protect information that is both sent and received between email servers. Transport-level security (TLS) encryption is the first method of protecting email communications. The email message is encrypted as it travels from the sender to the service provider's server, where it is briefly decrypted before being re-encrypted as it travels from the server to the recipient.

TLS encryption essentially converts a text message into a scrambled mess while traveling to and from the server. The point of possible risk is at the moment of the brief decryption while it's on the email server. The encryption doesn't last for the entire journey between the sender and receiver, so this presents security risks at the server level. The email service provider can read the information in the email, and third-party attacks on the server could result in data leaks and information vulnerability. Possible security risks and concerns regarding TLS encryption include:

- Protection being dependent on whether or not both parties in the communication have email providers that support TLS. Suppose the sender's provider supports it, but the recipient's doesn't. In that case, the protection is void, as the email is sent from the server to the recipient in a decrypted format.
- The email service provider being able to read your message, as it uses a public encryption key, which they hold. The provider may not be using this data with malicious intent, but instead may use it in order to show you personalized adverts or to auto-fill based on the language you often use. However, it's still an intrusion on your privacy.

Secure email service providers can help you negate this and several other vulnerabilities of unsecured email communication. There are many good secure email providers, and your choice will come down to personal preference. However, there are a few key features you should look for in a provider, listed here:

End-to-end encryption: Many secure email service providers negate the TLS pitfalls by offering users complete end-to-end encryption (E2EE). Users are assured that their email messages aren't decrypted at the server before being forwarded to the recipient. Not even the service provider can read the contents of your email. The message is encrypted on the sender's end and only gets decrypted once it reaches its destination.

Multifactor authentication: It's not just the content of your email while it's on the move between sender and recipient that can lead to breaches. Email account login breaches are also a serious threat. Creating a strong password does go a long way to prevent your login credentials from becoming compromised, but 2FA is the way to go to really make it difficult for criminals to succeed.

Server location: The provider's email server locations may have a significant impact on your privacy, due to entities such as government and law enforcement. For example, Five Eyes nations (Canada, United States, United Kingdom, New Zealand, and Australia) have a long-standing intelligence-sharing deal with each other, agreeing to grant each government the power to forcibly make any communication service provider do the following:

- Place malware in user devices
- Alter user experience of the service

- Disregard any current legislation in favor of the agreement
- Hand over user information under the direction of secret warrants
- Give governments any new product designs before they are approved for release

(Price, 2023)

The information gathered in one country is automatically permitted to be shared with the other countries in the agreement if it is requested. The governments can even place gag orders on service providers, preventing them from alerting their users to any breach of privacy. The Five Eyes nations then expanded their reach to form Nine Eyes, which incorporated Norway, Netherlands, France, and Denmark in the agreement. Since then, another five nations have come on board to form Fourteen Eyes, adding Sweden, Germany, Spain, Italy, and Belgium. Additionally, while not part of the Five, Nine, or Fourteen Eyes agreements, Singapore and Israel have special deals with the countries within these agreements. It's interesting to note that the nations included under Nine Eyes and Fourteen Eyes are sometimes held to different standards than the original Five Eyes nations. However, that doesn't mean your information is safe. Out of all the countries involved, the two safest options, although still not entirely secure, are Germany and Sweden.

Logs: Many email providers keep information logs, such as connection times and IP addresses. These logs can be used to garner information about communications and more. A good, secure email provider shouldn't store logs, but if you are given the option to do so, ensure both the amount of data logged, and how the information is stored, do not leave you open to maximum exposure.

Stripping metadata: Metadata is information about the data you possess and share. Email also has metadata, which could include information such as who you are sending the email to, what network and web browser you're using, or even details about your device. A secure email provider should strip the metadata.

Paid plans: Hosting an email service is usually costly, and it's never free. Many free email providers quietly gather information about you, your interests, and your activity. The information is used to show you advertisements from external parties who pay to have the ads displayed. Gathering various bits of information increases the chance of advertising success by targeting certain services and products toward you based on that information.

DATA BACKUPS

Backing up data means copying the information to a secondary storage location to safeguard it. The data types that can be backed up will range from documents and media files, such as images and videos, to operating systems, chat logs, and many others. Backing up your data is a vital part of any cybersecurity strategy for a few reasons:

Data loss: Losing data can take on various forms:

- The device on which the data is primarily stored could be stolen or misplaced.
- The device could be irreplaceably damaged, such as being dropped or damaged in a fire.
- A system crash could erase or damage the data.
- Hardware failure could damage or erase the data.
- Individual files or entire hard drives could become corrupt.
- Malicious damage from a cyber attack could erase or damage the data.

In the event of data loss for any reason, you will want to be able to retrieve essential information from a backup location. You'll be saved a lot of hassle and even heartache, and ensure you have peace of mind, if your sensitive information and digital memories are safe, should anything happen to the primary device they're saved on.

Data corruption: This is linked to data loss, but it goes a step further. Any hardware storage device or even digital storage system can become corrupted. You may need more than just one backup of your information to be protected from data loss. Backing your data up several times in different places or on other devices can avoid data loss if the first backup becomes corrupted.

Archiving: Backing up data allows you to create digital archives. You can keep old data neatly filed away for future reference or for keeping sentimental records and memories instead of having to delete them when your device storage capacity is running low.

Data Backup Tips

Backing up your data is more complex than simply copying it to a cloud or hard drive. Here are some tips to help you effectively and securely back everything up:

Protect your backed-up data: Use strong login credentials to access the backups. If possible, enable two-factor authentication (2FA) to increase data protection.

Control access to your backups: Using login credentials and 2FA doesn't protect your physical backup devices from theft, loss, or damage. If you use devices such as hard drives or USBs, keep them safely locked away to prevent them from falling into the wrong hands.

Use the 3-2-1 rule: This rule states that you should have three recent data backups. The first two backups should be done on different devices and can be stored in your home. The third backup should be stored off-site in a different location. Before cloud services emerged, this usually meant keeping a USB or hard drive in a safe location, such as at a trusted friend or family member's home. However, these days, you can make the third backup to a cloud or even to two cloud accounts if you really want to play it safe. The 3-2-1 rule ensures that if one of the two locally–stored backups is damaged or lost, there is a second one. However, suppose a disaster such as a flood or a fire damages both local backups. In that case, the third one keeps your data safe and available.

Perform regular backups: Regularly backing up your most important information is just as important as ensuring your backups are secure. Anything can happen at any time, and only backing up vital data once in a blue moon is a surefire way to lose data should something happen.

Encrypt your data: Data encryption is an additional layer of protection that renders your data unreadable should someone somehow get past your login credentials and 2FA. Both Windows and Mac devices have native programs that allow you to encrypt physical external storage devices. BitLocker is a Windows native application but may not be available on all machines or types of operating systems. For Mac, the app is called FileVault. There are also third-party applications that offer device encryption, but if you go the third-party route, ensure you use a verified and reputable provider.

Encrypt data on removable devices: Aside from external hard drives, data can be stored on various devices, including USBs and even SIM cards. In case of loss or theft of these devices, encryption can help keep personal information out of the wrong hands.

Data Disposal Tips

Data disposal is just as important for your information security as data backups are. You've put so much time and effort into securing your data that it makes no sense to ignore how to properly and safely dispose of data and storage devices you no longer need. Just because you don't need the data anymore doesn't mean it can't still be used by cybercriminals.

Make old data storage devices unreadable: It doesn't matter why you want to get rid of an old hard drive or storage device. Perhaps it's starting to glitch, or you've invested in a new computer. Simply deleting everything and emptying your recycle bin is the least secure way of cleaning up old data storage. Even formatting the hard drive before tossing or selling the device isn't enough to ensure your data is safe. Once you've transferred and backed up your data, it's imperative to completely wipe the slate clean. You can do this in one of three ways:

- **Magnetic cleaning:** Also called degaussing, this will likely destroy the hard drive and so should only be done if you want to render it completely unusable. Inside a hard drive are magnets that control the components that write and read the data on the drive. Running a powerful magnet repeatedly over the hard drive will corrupt, scramble, or erase the data on the hard drive or even annihilate the drive. A small magnet like a fridge magnet isn't strong enough to do the trick, and you should consider having a professional perform this task in order to ensure it's done correctly.
- **Hard drive disk shredding:** This method will, in no uncertain terms, entirely destroy the hard drive. The

device is literally put through a hard drive version of a paper shredder, physically grinding it to pieces. After the shredding, due to the physical destruction of the hard drive, the data cannot be put back together in any intelligible or useful way. This method is best left to professionals with the proper equipment to completely shred your old drives.

- **Data-wiping software:** You can use software from a third-party provider to sanitize and wipe your hard drive prior to selling it or giving it to someone else. This software deep–cleans and completely erases everything off the hard drive in such a way that it's not recoverable. It's critical to carefully choose the software and provider to ensure they're reputable and have good reviews.

Overwrite deleted data: When you move something to your recycle bin on a device, emptying the recycle bin doesn't actually delete the file. It stays on the hard drive until new data needs the space it's taking up, and it gets overwritten. When you're deleting sensitive files, they should be permanently deleted by being overwritten so they can't be retrieved before they are naturally overwritten. If you aren't particularly tech-savvy, you should approach an IT professional to assist you with overwriting a hard drive or removing deletions. This will ensure old, sensitive files are truly gone.

Don't forget about old backups: The old adage "Out of sight, out of mind." is often true of data. It's easy to forget, especially to online cloud services, what you have backed up and what you have not deleted or overwritten. Backups are extremely valuable, as we know. Still, having backups requires you to take extra steps when deleting old information. Anything you want to permanently delete from your local device should also be permanently removed from all backup locations; otherwise, it's not really gone for good.

WHAT'S NEXT?

Several principles for securing your accounts and information can be applied to your online activity. For example, secure login credentials should always be used for all social media accounts. However, having robust access control and authorization protocols will not necessarily be enough to keep your information and accounts safe. Convenient ways of online browsing, such as saving logins with the "remember me" function in your browser, might make logging into accounts quicker and easier, but they come with a compromise. In the next step, we'll delve into how your online browsing and social media interactions can be made more secure. From curating what you share online to learning to spot unsecured websites, navigating the cyber world is about to become more secure and more private, and safer for you.

CREATING A SAFER CYBERCOMMUNITY

Educating yourself about cybersecurity is only one piece of the information protection puzzle. It can be a large and complicated puzzle to piece together from start to finish, but you're already on your way to having a better understanding of cybersecurity.

Take a moment to really appreciate how far you've come in your understanding of cybersecurity and what it means to you, personally. Answer the following few questions to gauge your own progress:

Did any of the statistics and real-world stories shock you? Did you even know about any of them?

Did you find a deeper understanding of cybersecurity and cybercrime to be enlightening?

Were you aware of the legal and ethical aspects of cybersecurity and how compliance from organizations impacts you personally?

Maybe it's also come to your attention that many everyday users of information technology are unaware of the genuine threats they face. Maybe you have realized that you've been a target of attempted cybercrime before but didn't fully grasp the potential risk of the situation at the time. Understanding and grappling with this knowledge and these realizations can be both scary and a bit of a rude awakening. You are also now likely to be motivated to continue your own personal journey to better cybersecurity. However, cybersecurity is ultimately a concerted societal effort. As tight as your security measures may be, your efforts could well be compromised because others know information about you, but their cybersecurity knowledge and practices leave gaps for criminals to exploit.

Sharing the knowledge of cybersecurity is vital for your own protection. Educating your friends and family about cybersecurity, cybercrime, and the precautions everyone can take to make the digital world a safer place are crucial. But it doesn't stop there, because it's not just the people you know who could lead to a data breach that affects you. Considering the vastness of online connectedness globally, it could be anybody, anywhere.

Encouraging others to learn about cybersecurity and improve their protection benefits every person who interacts with technology. If you find the information valuable, consider sharing that knowledge and motivating others to learn more by leaving a review of this book. **By sharing your review, you help open others' eyes to the value of this information and encourage them to take that necessary step to educate themselves about the threats lurking in the digital shadows.**

Our mission is to spread as much knowledge and awareness to each everyday user as possible. Your help by reviewing what you're learning goes a long way to making this guide visible to more people.

Please check out the link below, or you can scan the QR code to leave feedback on Amazon.

https://www.amazon.com/review/create-review/?asin=1738431207

8

STEP 4: SECURE YOUR ONLINE BROWSING AND SOCIAL MEDIA

Cybercriminals aren't just trying to prise their way into your devices, networks, or accounts. They're also lying in wait for you as you browse online or interact with people on social media. From fake websites to fake social media profiles, their methods of trying to dupe you into giving them access to valuable information or glean sensitive data from your interactions are as varied as they are unscrupulous. Securing your online browsing and social media requires proper security protocols, tools, and heightened vigilance for the human element in attacks. Luckily, there are several easy-to-use security measures you can put in place, starting today, to make your navigation of the online realm and its interactions far safer.

ONLINE BROWSING CYBERSECURITY PRACTICES

While many of your accounts may be located online, surfing the web presents a different set of threats. Navigating the internet safely without the necessary cybersecurity practices is akin to sailing through a stormy sea without a compass. From pop-up ads to hidden malware, the risks are plentiful and can be hard to detect. However, that's not to say you can't make the internet a safer place to work and play. In this step of your cybersecurity guidance, we will cover the basics of making online browsing safer.

Some cybersecurity measures we've mentioned in previous steps apply to securing your online browsing, such as:

- Using a VPN
- Keeping your browsers up to date
- Avoiding using public Wi-Fi and networks

The same reasons for employing these measures when using your devices and networks also apply to online browsing. If you would like a refresher on these practices and why you need to include them in your cybersecurity strategy, head back to step 2 to review the more in-depth discussions.

That being said, there are numerous browser–specific measures you can use to tighten your browsing security, and that's what we're about to learn.

Use HTTPS Only Mode

If you look at the address bar at the top of your browser, you'll notice many websites have an online address that begins with 'http://' or 'https://'. The letters in 'http' stand for 'hypertext transfer protocol secure'. It's an online protocol that secures communication over the internet by encrypting any data being sent and received between the website and your browser. If a website is reputable, it will use HTTPS, making it a good indication of whether you can trust the website or not. You can often see the web address of a website on the search engine's search results page, right under the website's title or name. However, scrutinizing every web address before clicking on a search result isn't something most people are used to and is an unnecessary inconvenience. You can enable your browser's HTTPS–only mode in order to avoid inadvertently clicking on an unsecured site. Your browser will then only show you results from secured HTTPS websites and remove the potential risk of HTTP sites. Using only HTTPS sites is crucial when interacting with a website that requires your financial information, such as your credit card number.

Be Wary of Extensions

Browser extensions are very useful, and there are many of them available. Also sometimes called plug-ins, browser extensions add versatility and extra functions to your browser. The problem is that extension developers are as susceptible to security flaws as other developers. Extensions run the risk of being infected with malicious code, which goes to work as soon as you download and install the extension. To reduce the threat to your data, only use extensions you really need. If an extension would be nice to have but isn't necessary, opt to live without it. When you do need an extension, do some cyber sleuthing and pick one from a reputable developer who has been around for a while and has received good reviews.

Block Pop-ups

Have you ever clicked on a link, image, or video, only to have an unexpected browser window pop up, usually with some suspect content or suspicious advertisement? Pop-up windows can be incredibly annoying but also sinister. They can be a major gateway for malware attacks or for data harvesting, via criminal websites posing as legitimate ones. Most reputable browsers include the option to block these windows without having to install a third-party extension. Enabling this feature not only removes the annoyance and inconvenience of having to close the windows, but it also prevents you from accidentally clicking on a suspicious link or visiting a malicious website.

Use a Reliable Adblocker

An adblocker is a browser extension you definitely want to install. Adblockers are a somewhat controversial choice, because as well as blocking malicious advertisements and various other threats, they can also block legitimate websites that use them to earn money through paid advertising. Good adblockers allow you to customize what is blocked and what is allowed, so you can still support websites you trust by seeing their ads.

Be 'Cookie Conscious'

Cookies are everywhere on the web. The constant pop-up messages about cookie settings and cookie management can be frustrating. You need to know what cookies are, and why you should not just automatically click "accept all" in your bid to get to the content you want.

Cookies are pieces of data that websites gather and store in your browser. They include different kinds of information that can be used to gain insight into your online activity. Cookies, in themselves, aren't inherently malicious. They're designed to gather information that can be used to tailor your browsing experience to your preferences. For example, you may notice that ads, articles, and links to web pages you're shown are typically linked to your interests based on the websites that you visited and the products that you viewed. Cookies can also store user's data such as login credentials and much more. The integrity of a website plays a significant role in cookie security. Reputable, secure sites will encrypt personal cookie data to prevent third parties from accessing the information.

The problem with cookies, as helpful as they can be, is that they're attractive to cybercriminals. They can be used to impersonate you on a website, access your accounts, steal login credentials like passwords, and collect other sensitive information. Cookies are also a potential method for spreading malware. Your privacy can be compromised by tracking your online activity for user profiling. To lower the potential threat they pose to your cybersecurity and privacy, follow these simple cookie safety tips:

Browser control: Various browsers offer built-in cookie control preferences that allow you to customize settings to suit your preferences. You can select what kind of website data can be collected from how long the data is kept, such as until you shut down the browser or disable cookies entirely. You can also check your browser privacy settings and disable cookie data storage. Most major browsers have the settings feature to manage cookie permissions, including which sites can and can't collect data.

Extensions: If your browser doesn't offer you the option to fine-tune your cookie preferences, you can look into installing an extension. Remember to follow the tips for choosing extensions listed above.

Malware: Keep your malware and antivirus programs updated to nip potential cookie-related attacks in the bud.

Cookie management: Most websites these days inform you that they use cookies and provide you with the options of either managing the specific data collected, rejecting all cookies, or accepting all cookies. Resist the temptation to click "accept all". If you aren't given the option to reject all cookies, take a moment to review what data is being collected and deactivate what you're not comfortable with.

Legitimacy: If the website you visit or the cookie settings they offer don't seem legitimate or make you unsure of your safety, stop browsing immediately and exit.

Delete: You can get rid of unwanted cookies by navigating to your browser's privacy settings and cleaning out your old, unwanted cookies.

Install a Password Manager

This is another extension you should consider for improving your browsing security. A large number of websites and accounts with logins now offer you the option to remember the password for quick and easy auto-login. This may be convenient, but a website's built-in password management system isn't always as safe as you or the website would like to imagine it to be. Ultimately, the safest option is simply not to store passwords and login information, but it's not always convenient. For better password protection while still having easy access to your passwords, consider a reputable third-party password manager. Choose a password manager in the same way you would any other extension, according to the tips listed earlier in the chapter, but also keep an eye out for two-factor authentication. Having 2FA vastly increases the level of protection the extension offers.

Browse Privately

The private browsing option, also known as incognito mode, is often mistaken for completely untracked browsing. Unfortunately, this isn't what's happening. When you choose private browsing, your activity may still be tracked but the information about your activity during that browsing session is deleted when you shut down the browser window. This includes your history, downloads, and cookies. Some private browsers may rigidly restrict activity tracking. Private browsing is one way to ensure your online activity isn't recorded, and cookies aren't stored from your session. It's extremely useful for protecting your privacy if you use a shared device or public computer or want to visit a website from which you don't want cookies stored.

Disable Autofill

The autofill feature presents you with a choice between convenient browsing and cybersecurity. It's meant to help you fill in certain types of regularly used information quickly. It's similar to choosing the "remember me" native password management system that many websites use, but it includes more information than just your login credentials for a specific website or account. The information collected for autofill includes names, email addresses, physical addresses, and even financial information. There are two significant concerns about this feature, which should be all the motivation you need to pass up the convenience and disable autofill:

- Anyone who accesses your device can retrieve the saved information.
- Cybercriminals can trick you into quickly and easily giving up sensitive information on a fake or malicious online form.

Sign Up for Activity Notifications

These notifications don't prevent activity from happening on your account if someone has your legitimate login or verification credentials. They do, however, alert you to unauthorized activity, such as purchases or transfers, which allows you to take quick action against the breach.

Only Shop on Trusted Websites

There are thousands of online shopping portals offering a dizzying array of products. However, not all online retail portals are created equal and, therefore, they do not all share the same level of consumer privacy protection measures. Only transact on websites you trust or with a good reputation and glowing reviews. If anything seems awry or potentially sinister, stop shopping before you provide payment details and find the product somewhere else.

Use a Secure Browser

Browsers vary in the features they offer, including the levels of safety and security. To ensure you are taking the maximum precautions to secure your online activity, consider using a secure browser. These browsers employ additional security measures to safeguard your privacy. You can think of a browser as a bicycle that will take you around the internet. A secure browser is like a bicycle with all the protective bells and whistles like a crash helmet, goggles, body protectors, and knee and elbow guards. It's important to note that even with all these safety extras, you're not guaranteed never to get hurt. Still, they certainly will keep you a lot safer.

Features to look for in a secure browser include:

Blocking pop-ups: Pop-ups originating from secure or trusted websites aren't necessarily safe and could redirect users to malicious websites. Blocking all pop-ups, even the legitimate ones, improves security.

Sandboxing: Sandboxing means that malicious applications or code is contained and not allowed to run rampant. It's similar to how a child's sandbox keeps the sand in a confined area where it can't contaminate everything else.

Blocking crypto mining: Cybercriminals know that the mining for cryptocurrency takes up much of a device's power and capability. Some illegal cryptocurrency miners have learned how to hijack an unsuspecting victim's device to do their dirty work, taking up all the hijacked device's system resources instead of slowing down their own devices.

Plugin security: Plugins, or extensions, as we know, are helpful additional features to improve the diversity of browser functionality without the browser developers having to put in the work to create and offer them. Not all extensions apply to all browsers, and many are browser-specific. Secure browsers only allow approved, safe plugin developer products to be installed.

Blocking tracking: Tracking can be done via cookies or scripts. The aim is to provide websites with information about your online activity so they can show you targeted ads based on your activity to increase their chances of earning revenue from the advertisers. Blocking tracking improves the privacy of your online activity.

Blocking JavaScript: Various websites run code in the JavaScript programming language in the background to enable website interactive features such as pop-up ads and videos to run. Unfortunately, while these features improve the interactive nature of the internet, they are susceptible to hacking by cybercriminals. Blocking JavaScript prevents malicious code from running in the background while you browse a website.

HTTPS-only mode: HTTPS is an effective security upgrade on the standard HTTP protocol. A secure browser should allow you to enable the HTTPS-only mode, preventing you from accidentally accessing unsecured websites.

SOCIAL MEDIA CYBERSECURITY PRACTICES

Social media takes on many forms, and many people have multiple "socials", taking advantage of different platforms for their unique features or appeal. Different social media platforms are designed to target different kinds of audiences. The popularity of using multiple platforms can be seen in the option to cross-post between them and share content from one to another. In many ways, social media has largely replaced other kinds of social interaction, such as phone calls and email.

Social media allows us to connect with one another, see what our friends and family are up to, promote ourselves professionally, buy and sell things, and so much more. It's important to remember that all of this activity is being carried out on an online stage for all the world to see, and that can be risky. More of your personal information is readily available to the online public than ever before.

This abundance of public information poses a considerable threat to your privacy and security. In addition to your information being out there, social media platforms are a cybercriminal's playground. Here's how to be cybersecurity-conscious while still enjoying the perks of social media.

Protect Your Login

Login protection is one of the most basic cybersecurity practices for any online account. Social media is no exception. One of the first steps to take toward securing your account login is to ensure you are creating a strong password and following good password hygiene. Having covered this in step 3, do refer back to the section on passwords to ensure your social media passwords and practices meet the bar. You can also employ various browsing cybersecurity measures mentioned in the previous section, such as not using autofill and using a password manager. Additional login protection tips to stop unauthorized access to your accounts include:

Logging out of any social media accounts when you're not using them: This may seem inconvenient compared to simply clicking on a bookmark or opening an app where your account is already logged in, but this means that anyone who uses your devices will also have the same automatic access to your accounts.

Never logging in using links: Whether there's a link on a website that will take you to a social media platform or you're sent a link from someone, never use a link to log in. Links can direct you to false login pages where cybercriminals can steal your login credentials when you enter them. They can then access your account and wreak havoc by impersonating you to cause reputational damage, exploit your relationships, and more.

Check Your Privacy Settings

Social media platforms offer users control over their privacy through privacy settings. These settings let you decide what to share with whom, and they let you decide who can see what information about you. Different platforms offer different levels of control based on how the users interact. Some examples of the kinds of information you can make public or private include:

- Personal information such as birthdays and contact details
- Information from your social media posts and feed
- Posts you are tagged in that show up on your feed/timeline
- Your friends list and who can see it
- Individual posts. These can be made private or public at the time of posting

Be sure to carefully comb through your privacy settings for each platform and restrict visibility according to your personal preferences. Sometimes, sharing more information is beneficial, such as if you are leveraging social media for professional purposes. However, look at each feature that can be controlled and ask yourself these questions:

- Why am I making this information visible to anyone who isn't a friend or family member?
- What is the value of publicizing this information instead of keeping it set to private or, even better, not posting it at all?
- Will making this information private negatively affect me in any way?
- What malicious activities could be perpetrated with this information if it remains public? This includes your information being used falsely or to contact you as part of a social engineering attack. Even potentially innocent information, such as pages and groups you like or are part of, can be used against you. For example, a cybercriminal could use your phone number and a group you are part of, contact you pretending to be someone from that group, and get you to divulge valuable information. Think about that carefully and let it sink in.

Tip: Check your privacy settings regularly. Social media platforms regularly roll out updates and tweaks to their user interface and systems. Unlike other apps, these updates are usually automatically applied without giving you notice until after the update has been actioned. Sometimes, tweaks and updates can result in settings being changed. Regularly confirm your privacy settings to make sure nothing has changed to potentially expose your information without your knowledge.

Put the Internet on an Information Diet

Avoid sharing anything about yourself, your family, or your work online unless it is absolutely necessary. If you do want to share information, carefully consider whether anything you are sharing could be used against you in any way. Even something as innocent as sharing holiday snaps online can contribute to identity theft. Be particularly wary of sharing any personally identifying information online, such as the full names of anyone, contact details, and personally sensitive information.

Important note: Anything you post to social media or on the internet stays there *forever*. Over time, it may become more difficult to find, but it's still there. Keep that in mind whenever you post anything, and consider how this data could affect you years or even decades down the line.

Make Posts Private

If you aren't big on garnering public attention or making your opinion known to the world, it's worth considering protecting your social media posts on all platforms. As with all forms of social media, posts can be used to skim information. Minimize your risk of cyberattack by making your posts private so that only approved followers can see them.

Curate Your Posts for Your Online Reputation

Your online reputation can reach a wider audience than you are aware of. What you post online is no longer separate from your personal or professional representation of yourself. Even old accounts and posts you've forgotten about can come back to haunt you in the present or future. Carefully curate all your online information and posts to exclude any potentially harmful representation that could impact your social and professional success. If you aren't sure if posting something could negatively impact you now or in the future, don't post it. For example, posting suggestive gym or beach photos to your personal social media accounts could be found years later and result in you being turned down from or losing a dream job.

Make Friends Wisely

Friends can be made on social media through various means. Sometimes, a platform will suggest people to befriend or it will suggest accounts for you to follow based on people you are already friends with or accounts you already follow. The upside to this is that it can connect you with people you may know, and with people you might want to get to know. Another method is to actively befriend or follow another person or account. If you are using social media for purely personal purposes, to keep up with your nearest and dearest, a good rule of thumb is to only accept requests or suggestions from people you actually know. This isn't a completely secure practice, but it goes a long way to avoiding "friending" a malicious account. When you receive a friend request, there are a few questions to ask yourself before accepting:

- Do you know this person in real life?
- Accepting requests from people you know in real life (and discarding requests from people you don't know), goes a long way to preventing you from accepting a request from a scammer. Once you accept the friend request, the scammer will have access to your private or non-public information, exposing the information you're trying to protect to potential threats.
- Do you have any mutual friends?
- If you don't recognize the person the request is from, but you have mutual friends, they may be reaching out to grow their social network. If you have mutual friends, it may be worthwhile messaging the profile before accepting to ascertain who they are, how they know you or your mutual friends, and why they want to be your friend.
- If you do have mutual friends, how many are there?
- The more mutual friends you have with another person or profile, the more likely the request will be genuine. Scammer profiles can but rarely do share many mutual friends. The more friends you have on a particular account, the more mutual friends you

should expect to have before considering accepting the request. Again, if you need more clarification, you can message the profile as suggested above to get some answers.

Just because you don't know a profile or have any mutual friends doesn't mean the friend request is innately malicious. Here are some options of what to do if you get a request from a profile you don't share any mutual friends with:

- **Decline and block:** If you are confident you will not benefit from this friendship and don't feel like investigating further, decline the request and block the account from contacting you again.
- **Investigate:** People can find your account if you are in the same group or community, like the same pages, or by the @ and # tags you use. If you are curious and want to investigate, go to the profile. The following may be indications of a fake or scam profile account:
- An avatar as a profile image
- A low-resolution human profile image
- Very few friends or followers
- A newly created account (hours, days, weeks, or even only a few months old)
- Few to no posts
- No common groups, likes, or interests
- A suspicious location
- Poor spelling, grammar, and sentence structure

- A profile image that doesn't match an ethnic/traditional name, occupation, or overall "feel" of the profile information

Ultimately, it's up to you to decide who may or may not be legitimate, and after doing some investigating of the potential friend, all you can do is trust your instinct. However, take the above list into consideration and use extreme discretion before accepting requests from anyone you don't know and don't have mutual friends with.

Important note: Even if you get a friend request from someone you know, it could still be a scam or a duplicate profile or a fake account. If you are already friends with the person online and receive a second request, it may be a duplicate scam account. Whether you are friends on social media or not, it's worth contacting the person outside of social media to confirm they are the one who sent you the request. A duplicate account could be a scam, but it could also be legitimate if the person's original account was hacked and they resorted to creating a new one.

Beware Strange Messages

Social media accounts can be hacked. It happens all the time. Often, suspicious activity on the account happens before the rightful account owner becomes aware they've been hacked. Whenever you get social media messages from a trusted friend, scrutinize the message. If anything seems "off" about the message, reach out to the person via another channel to confirm the message really came from them. Indications of potential hacker messages include:

- Different language use
- Unusual spelling, grammar, or sentence structure mistakes
- Strange requests that seem out of character, such as for money or asking for personal information the person isn't entitled to or should already know
- Requests for help involving sensitive information such as one-time-PINs that, it may be claimed by a cybercriminal, have been sent to your number or email by mistake.

Important note: Social engineering cyber attacks can seem entirely legitimate. Approach any messages requesting any kind of information with a healthy amount of speculation.

Sign Up for Login Notifications

If someone lays their grubby malicious hands on your account login credentials and manages to successfully log into the account, you may never know. Signing up for notifications of logins on unknown devices gives you a heads-up so you can act sooner rather than later.

Clean Up Your Profile

Many people like pages and join groups that align with their interests. Sometimes, interests change over time. Groups and pages are susceptible to infiltration by cybercriminals. Reduce your risk of social media attacks by limiting the number of pages and groups you are part of or follow. Regularly perform a profile clean-up by unliking and unfollowing pages and groups you aren't committed to participating in anymore. Between limiting likes and limiting what you follow, you reduce the avenues of opportunistic attack you are exposing yourself to.

Beware Links and Attachments

Links and attachments can be sent and shared on social media in various ways. They can be shared to people's profiles, offered as ads or content of interest through third-party advertisements, or sent through private messages.

Aside from the above indicators of potentially harmful messages, avoid clicking on any links sent to you via social media. A malicious message can come from either someone you know or someone you don't know. The messages may not appear suspicious, but if they contain a link, be cautious, as the link could be infected with malware or be part of a phishing attack. If you know the person the message came from, contact them via an alternative method to confirm the message and link are legitimate. If the message comes from an unknown profile, then ignore it and delete it.

If the link or attachment is shared by a profile, either contact the person via another channel to check the link's security, or simply scroll past. It can come across as overbearingly paranoid if you contact your friends and family for every single link they share on their social feed. So, if you aren't absolutely sure you will lose sleep over not clicking the link, just ignore it.

Third-party advertisements for products, brands, or services are always risky to click on. If you are interested in what's being offered, search for it directly in your browser. You can search directly for the article's manufacturer or for the supplier's official website. These are both a more secure way of finding what you're interested in.

Beware of Competitions and Questionnaires

Many competitions and questionnaires are legitimate, but many could be a ploy to gather information or initiate a malware attack. Whenever you enter a competition or fill out a questionnaire online, carefully consider what personal information they are asking you for. The risks involved in filling out forms for competitions or questionnaires include:

- Potentially clicking on malicious links
- Providing information that could be gathered and used in a cyber attack or sold to another malicious party
- Providing information that could be used in an exploitation attack where a ransom needs to be paid to prevent the information being made public

Delete Old Accounts

Everything online is constantly in flux and in a state of continual change. This includes social media. There are old social media platforms that only some people ever use anymore. You may have moved on from an old account or platform, but that doesn't mean your profile simply disappears into the abyss of internet vastness. Once the information is on the internet, it's there to stay, unless measures are taken to remove it, or measures are taken to prevent unauthorized access. MySpace was a social media platform that preceded Facebook. Many people who had MySpace accounts but transitioned to Facebook probably haven't deleted those old MySpace accounts. MySpace is still around online, and those accounts are potentially still accessible. The same goes for changing accounts on the same platform. The old accounts are still there, with potentially vulnerable information. If you have old social media accounts you no longer use, for whatever reason, log in and delete the accounts to prevent them from being hacked, impersonated, or the information used illegally.

EXTRA CYBERSECURITY TIPS

Beware of eavesdroppers: When you're out and about, anybody around you could be a potential eavesdropper. People around you can listen to your conversations in person or over the phone. Additionally, a visual form of eavesdropping, sometimes called "shoulder surfing," could put your information at risk. Whenever out in public, be aware of those around you who could be listening in or looking over your shoulder as you interact online via messaging, email, logging into accounts, or shopping online.

Use a wireless proximity alarm system: The system connects a wireless proximity device you keep on your person to your mobile device, such as a smartphone. If the device moves more than a certain distance away from the corresponding gadget on your person, an alarm sounds to let you know. These systems may not prevent the outright theft of a device, but you will instantly be reminded if you've left your device unattended or if it's been snatched. If you are unlucky enough not to be able to recover a stolen device, at least you will be able to take immediate action to reduce the amount of damage resulting from the incident.

Avoid downloading files from the internet: The internet is a treasure trove of free content from images and videos to software and much more. If you can access the content more safely, such as when making purchases on official websites, or when directly sharing through more secure channels, you should avoid downloading files from the internet. Peer-to-peer file-sharing platforms are hugely popular for quickly and easily accessing files, but they come with considerable risk. Any file could be infected with malware, even if the user who uploaded it is trusted or the platform the file came from has a good reputation.

Use official apps instead of your browser when on your mobile devices: The official apps for a variety of providers, such as financial institutions, are designed to have greater security than browser access. Wherever possible, opt to use official apps instead of transacting through your browser when you're on a mobile device.

Use different email addresses for different categories of accounts: This tip works on the same principle as not using the same password for every account. Avoid using one email address across all accounts, from social media to shopping online. Instead, group accounts by context and use different email addresses to sign into different account categories. You can divide accounts into categories, such as financial, social media, professional, online retail, etc. This means you can use the same email address for Facebook and Instagram but use a different one for Amazon and other online shopping accounts.

Avoid signing up to websites using social media accounts: Many websites offer the option to sign up using your established social media or Google accounts. This may seem convenient, but it also increases the risk of your data being accessed unlawfully. These third-party sites often collect your details and stipulate that you need to grant them access to the information contained within these accounts. Even if you have your privacy settings locked down, if you comply with the malicious request, this loophole could throw all of that out the window because you could be signing up to a fake website and granting a cybercriminal access to your data.

WHAT'S NEXT?

So far, you've learned the essential tools and practices to improve your cybersecurity, from securing your devices and networks, to safeguarding your accounts and information. In this last step, you have gained the knowledge you need in order to stay protected in a world that revolves around social media and while surfing the web. You now know almost everything you need to improve and maintain a strict cybersecurity strategy. The emphasis is on "almost". From the start, we've learned how cybercrime has a vital human element, and nowhere is it more evident than in the prevalence and efficacy of social engineering attacks. In the next step, we'll discuss social engineering, and look at how it relates to cybersecurity, and also how to prevent falling victim to this popular attack method.

9

STEP 5: SOCIAL ENGINEERING – EVERYTHING YOU NEED TO KNOW

You may or may not have heard the term "social engineering". It applies to various crimes, not just cybercrime, and you may already have been a victim of it, even if you didn't know what it was called at the time.

As is shown by the Information Systems Audit and Control Association (ISACA) and LookingGlass, social engineering attacks consistently top the list of cybercrime as the leading method of attack in cybercrime. As of 2022, it's the most widely used tactic, and it's not all that surprising considering its efficacy (Crane, 2023).

WHAT IS SOCIAL ENGINEERING?

Social engineering is based on manipulation and exploitation of the fact that we're human and we make mistakes. It doesn't necessarily depend on how intelligent a person is, but purely that human error exists, and a person can quite often be manipulated into making the mistakes by cybercriminals. You can think of social engineering as computer hacking methods being replaced with "human hacking" techniques. Social engineering doesn't just happen in cybercrime and isn't always planned, though. It can occur in person and be a crime of opportunity. For example, a criminal could notice you've left your car door unlocked or slip into a secure property as the gate closes behind someone who has just legitimately entered. However, we will focus on the information technology side of social engineering as it pertains to your cybersecurity strategy.

Social engineering attacks come in different formats, including online, face-to-face, or over the phone, to name a few. They are often called scams, and cybercriminals exploit human thought and behavior patterns. The aim is to discover the motivation behind the behavior of a specific individual or a group of people and then use that motivation to manipulate them through deception. Another critical factor in the success of social engineering attacks is the need for more knowledge or awareness. Here, a lack of knowledge doesn't mean a lack of intellect. It means that a user may lack the knowledge or awareness of various types of cyberattacks, cybercrime trends, or the value of seemingly innocent personal information. This lack of awareness and understanding of the cybercrime landscape often leaves people vulnerable. It makes them more trusting and less suspicious.

How Do Social Engineering Attacks Work?

There are two common purposes of a social engineering attack:

1. Information, valuables, or money to be stolen from the victim.
2. Harm to be caused to the victim via financial, physical, or reputational damage.

The goal is to exploit human error by manipulating thoughts and behaviors. For this, most of these kinds of attacks require communication between cybercriminals and their victims. Most social engineering attacks follow a simple yet effective pattern or cycle that can be adapted to a variety of different situations, like a template. The format of the attack usually looks like this:

1. **Preparation:** Attackers spend time gathering as much useful information about the victim or a larger group they belong to. If the technique involves impersonation, the criminal may also investigate and collect information about the person or entity they intend to impersonate.
2. **Infiltration:** Attackers contact their victim and try to establish a relationship or rapport and gain trust. This part of the cycle can take anywhere from a few minutes to days, weeks, or even months, depending on what the criminal is trying to achieve.

3. **Exploitation:** Once the attacker has gained the victim's trust and determined their weaknesses in terms of human error, they exploit them to pull off the attack and get what they want.
4. **Disengagement:** After the attacker successfully gets what they want, they make their exit and move on to the next victim.

It's important to remember that these types of attacks aren't just about getting the victim to divulge valuable, sensitive information. They could also be used to initiate other forms of cyber attacks, such as getting the victim to open themselves up to exposure to malware. Impersonation is also popular in social engineering attacks targeting either individuals or organizations. Criminals could masquerade as employees of a legitimate organization to gain information from individuals. Alternatively, they could impersonate an individual to gain information about the person they're pretending to be. Either way, only a few pieces of information are needed to convince someone to hand over or confirm information.

IDENTIFY COMMON SOCIAL ENGINEERING CHARACTERISTICS

There are several characteristics common to the vast majority of social engineering attacks that aid in their success. Aside from the attacker needing to be versed in the art of persuasion, they will also need an abundance of confidence. You must be able to identify common SE attack traits to avoid falling victim to them. These include:

Emotional manipulation: There are few driving forces as powerful for prompting action as emotions. The stronger the emotion an attacker can evoke from their victim, the more likely they will succeed. Heightened emotions tend to cloud judgment and encourage risk-taking. A cybercriminal can try to elicit one or a combination of different emotions for better effect. These emotions may include:

- Anger
- Curiosity
- Excitement
- Fear
- Guilt
- Sadness

Whenever you are interacting with someone, pay close attention to your emotions. If the communication seems like it's trying to elicit emotion from you, take a step back to evaluate what you are being asked for or prompted to do. If it seems suspicious, disengage.

Trust: The ability to be trusted and the appearance of credibility go hand-in-hand. That is to say, the more credible and believable an attacker appears, the more likely they are to be trusted. Trust, once built, can also make the attacker seem more believable without being second-guessed.

During the preparation phase of the attack, a criminal will gather as much information as possible to make themselves appear as credible as possible so their narrative doesn't set any alarm bells ringing. Alternatively, they'll spend time gaining your trust and gathering information without rousing your suspicions when they finally deploy their main attack.

This characteristic can be tricky to spot in some instances, especially if the communication has been ongoing. However, many SE attacks are relatively short in duration and rely on impersonation to gain a level of trust. If someone is asking you for information or to do something, consider whether you can really trust them. If the trust results from claiming authenticity, such as being a representative from your financial institution, think about how they can prove they really are who they say they are. If you cannot confirm the information you require, disengage.

A sense of urgency: Urgency can make people think irrationally, especially when they're in a state of heightened emotions. Most social engineering attacks involve a time-sensitive aspect, whether it's a request or offering the victim an opportunity. By putting a time limit on the window for taking the action they want you to take, they create a sense of urgency that motivates risk-taking, possibly without the victim stopping to think things through more clearly. Examples of urgency include:

- A prize or reward being offered that can only be collected within a short amount of time, achieved by clicking on a link or providing information.
- A severe problem is fabricated, such as an account being closed or a device being infected with malware, and the problem is alleged to be only remedied with immediate action to prevent loss, damage, or inconvenience.

If any communication, from a pop-up to an email to a phone call, comes with a time-sensitive call to action, be wary. If you feel prompted to act quickly due to a perceived threat or loss of a reward, take time to think. If the communication is unsolicited, and especially if it comes from an unrecognized source, avoid following through with the action or providing the information requested. For example, if you are running antivirus software when a random pop-up window from an unknown source exclaims your device is infected, it's likely to be a scam, since your antivirus hasn't notified you of anything.

As with all things, there are always exceptions to the rule. Some social engineering attacks exploit personal human error that doesn't require contacting the victim. Such methods aim to use eavesdropping tactics such as listening into conversations and phone calls and "shoulder surfing" (where opportunistic criminals attempt to unassumingly spy over a victim's shoulder while they use their laptops, tablets, or other devices). Due to the wide range of social engineering attack methods, you may be asking how you can spot such attacks to avoid falling prey to these socially aware criminals.

The first step to spotting social engineering attacks is knowing what the different types of attacks are.

KNOW THE TYPES OF COMMON SOCIAL ENGINEERING ATTACKS

Since cybercrime is forever evolving and adapting to newfound vulnerabilities, nobody can ever confidently produce an extensive and all-encompassing list of the types of attacks that may occur. This is particularly significant to note as most cybercrime involves an element of social engineering. When you break it down to the basics, social engineering exploits human error, and human error can be made in almost any cyberattack situation. From unwittingly visiting fake and malicious websites to clicking on legitimate ads infected with external malware, to the more conventional forms of social engineering attacks, the human element is an influencing factor. However, it is possible to monitor trends and come up with a list of the most common and widely used methods built on social constructs.

From digital attacks to phone calls to face-to-face interaction, here's what to look for when identifying common social engineering attacks:

Phishing Attacks

We briefly touched on the different types of phishing attacks. Now it's time to address this very common cybercrime, what it looks like, and how to protect yourself. Phishing is the process a cybercriminal employs. The criminal lures their victim in the hope of getting a response. As such, this type of attack can be divided into two major categories:

Spam phishing: You can heed the name of this type of phishing attack by looking at the word "spam". Spam usually refers to unsolicited communication that generally targets a large group of recipients simultaneously. This is the most generic, least personalized, and most "luck-based" form of phishing. Typically, the attacker banks on sending out a high volume of simple, almost effortless, attack attempts on the assumption that the more messages sent, the more likely it is that a victim will be found.

Targeted phishing: This includes spear phishing and whale phishing, where specific individuals or organizations are targeted. Targeted phishing attacks require a more profound knowledge of the individual, group, or organization which the attacker is assaulting. To make targeted phishing more successful, an attacker must expend much more energy and time researching their victim to make the ploy more believable.

To be reminded of phishing attack channels, refer back to section 1, where the following types of phishing are explained:

- SMS phishing (Smishing)

- Voice phishing via phone calls (Vishing)

In addition to these types of phishing attacks, there are a few more you need to be aware of that don't have trendy "nicknames". These are:

Email phishing: This is the most traditional phishing type, and for good reason. It does not cost an attacker money, time, or significant effort to send an email, especially in comparison to sending an SMS or making a phone call. It can be done on a large scale, and the same message can be sent to every target.

Social media angling: As the name suggests, this attack subtype happens on social media platforms. In section 4, under 'Securing Your Social Media', we mentioned being wary of contact from both unknown profiles and even friends for just this reason. Attackers imitate a trusted profile, group, or page to get you to interact with them and provide them with the information they're after so they can take their malicious intentions further.

Search engine phishing: This is a process by which cyber-criminals attempt to undermine a user's trust in search engine results by replacing legitimate website result listings with fake ones. They may specifically target the paid result ads appearing first on the search results page to take advantage of the trust that users have in the legitimacy of these result links.

URL phishing: This kind of phishing attack can be administered in different ways, including email, SMS, social media messages, and even online advertisements. Attackers either send users links to click on or the attackers hijack legitimate online ads. Once a victim clicks the link, they are diverted to a fake website or the victims unknowingly download malware.

In-session phishing: These attempts interrupt your regular browsing experience of a legitimate website. They generally take the form of pop-ups prompting fake logins to keep you browsing the content you are interested in.

Identifying and avoiding common phishing attacks

Due to the array of types of phishing attacks, it can be difficult to identify every single one. However, there are a few traits to watch out for that can help keep you vigilant. Irrespective of how you are contacted and by whom, keep an eye out for the following:

First-time contact: Unsolicited communication from anyone is always a "red flag". Contact can be made over text, email, social media, or even phone calls. It would be prudent to imagine how this person got your email address, phone number, or other contact details. If you've never contacted this communication source, try to think why they are suddenly reaching out to you. It is wise to be wary.

Bad language protocols: Unfortunately, many phishing cyberattacks originate from people whose native language is not yours. Poor spelling, grammar, and sentence structure are usually good indicators of an attacker trying to make contact. When impersonating someone you know or a service provider you use, poor or unusual language use should be taken seriously. No professional organization will make such noticeable mistakes, especially in an age where services such as Grammarly are available to polish professional communications by reputable companies.

Generic greetings: Text-based phishing attacks are usually mass-produced for the criminal's convenience. Therefore, they will often use the most generic greeting possible that applies to the broadest audience. Although many professional organizations do use generic greetings, it's a good idea to be suspicious and investigate further to determine the legitimacy of the communication.

Urgent calls to action: These could be time-sensitive rewards or problem-solving prompts to outright threats. No friend or professional organization will ever employ either of such tactics. As discussed, urgency is a characteristic of many SE attacks. Threats are a clear giveaway of malicious intent, especially in combination with other phishing characteristics. For example, if the communication includes a generic greeting, impersonal communication, and no reference to any specific websites that could indicate knowledge of your personal online activity, it's probably fake and relying on your panic to cloud your critical thinking.

Email domains that don't match up: This isn't just email-specific and can be applied to SMS and even phone communication. Always scrutinize the email domain or phone number that the communication originates from. Lots of spam phishing communication comes from attackers who can't be bothered to spoof domains or numbers. It can be so poorly constructed that the domain or number doesn't match up at all. However, the attack can be sophisticated enough to only include a tiny deviation from a sender or organization's legitimate domain or number. Double and triple-check domains and numbers if you suspect phishing.

Avoiding Phishing Attempts

Despite your cybersecurity strategy, such as using secure email providers that include anti-phishing features, there is always a risk of being exposed to this kind of attack. Here's how to avoid falling prey to an attack if it sneaks past your security measures:

If an email or pop up or advertisement or request for information seems suspicious, investigate further. Here are some useful suggestions:

- Check email domains.
- Check official organization phone numbers or search the number that the message or call came from.
- End the call and opt to contact the organization via a publicized official contact number to query the contact/reward/threat instead.
- Never click on any attachments or links in emails or other message formats, unless you completely trust the legitimacy of the communication.

- If communication from someone you know seems unusual in any way, always contact the person via another channel to confirm the source of the communication (whether you are using social media message, text message, email, or another form of communication).
- Delete and ignore any obviously suspicious communication; there's no point in holding onto useless, failed cyberattack attempts.

How to Spot Other Social Engineering Attack Subtypes

Many of the following types of social engineering cyber-crime are based on phishing methodology. Therefore, it's worth applying your knowledge of the traits of phishing attacks when considering whether you are being manipulated into pandering to the desires of a cybercriminal.

Baiting attacks: Curiosity is a victim's downfall in this type of attack. The lure to pique your interest could be any reward that sates your curiosity. Bait can include:

Email or message attachments or links, which are often accompanied by an enticing message. Messages to lure you in can include:

- "You won't believe this!"
- "Have you seen this?"
- "Have you seen this photo of you?"
- "Limited time offer", "act quickly" (or other time-sensitive prompts).

- "Free" (with the request that you "click here now" or "enter [x, y, z information] to receive free [product or reward]"

Another form of baiting attack is called a quid pro quo attack. An attacker tries to lure the victim into providing information in return for a reward. Most commonly, these kinds of attacks are presented in the context of one-time offers, competitions, or giveaways.

Baiting attacks can be delivered via email, messages, phone calls, or website pop-up offers. If you ever feel you are being encouraged to click a link or provide any information, be wary. If you want to sign up for something free or click a link, try to confirm the authenticity of the source of the communication or their reputation. Remember, even legitimate, reputable websites can have their newsletter pop-up window hijacked by cybercriminals.

Pretext attacks: The name of the game with these kinds of attacks is establishing trust on the pretext of the attacker impersonating a trusted channel of contact. Communication for pretext attacks requires the criminal has knowledge of the victim, or of a legitimate organization, so that the criminal can appear to have legitimate contact credentials, for example. The attacker is trying to convince you they are legitimate on the pretext of their narrative, and the veracity of what they know about you or about the entity they are impersonating by way of their apparent contact credentials. To avoid pretext attacks, consider why you feel inclined to trust the source of the communication, whether their authenticity can be verified, and what you are being asked to do or provide.

SOCIAL ENGINEERING ATTACK CHECKLIST

Keeping up to date with the trends of social engineering attacks and their characteristics can be confusing. Here's a rundown of red flags to keep an eye out for:

- Do you know the person or entity the communication claims to be from?
- Does the domain or number that the communication is from match the actual person or entity's official or known contact details?
- Is there something strange or suspicious about the website's URL, language, wording, or logos?
- Does the communication:

1. Express urgency or time-sensitivity
2. Try to play to your emotions
3. Have bad or unusual spelling, grammar, or sentence structure
4. Offer a reward in return for providing information about yourself
5. Contain a threat to prompt you to take immediate action

- Double-check legitimacy, including comparing social media links to official or known social media and contact details for friends and organizations. Any discrepancy, even a single letter, number, or symbol, can be telling.
- Confirm any suspicious communication with friends, family, co-workers, or networking professionals via alternative communication channels to the method you received the contact. For example, phone a friend you got a message from or use the official customer service number to confirm contact from an organization instead of replying to a message or email.
- Apply the principle of "If it sounds too good to be true, it probably is." to any offer or opportunity you receive.
- Ask for proof of authentic identity. If someone cannot prove their legitimacy to your suspicion-fueled satisfaction, it's better to investigate and authenticate the contact by other means, even if their request has a pressing sense of urgency.

WHAT'S NEXT?

You should give yourself a pat on the back right now. You've made it through the majority of the steps needed to achieve the best cybersecurity practices. Your security and privacy, while interacting with information technology, will both improve. So far, you've stuck with it and meticulously investigated and amended your current cybersecurity basics according to the steps suggested in this guide. You've covered your bases, so to speak. However, there is a little more security legwork to be done. Get ready for some additional tips for making your cybersecurity as effective as possible.

INCREASING GLOBAL CYBERSECURITY

You've come so far in your journey to better cybersecurity that you're probably feeling less and less vulnerable each time you use connected technology. It's perhaps a sobering thought to contemplate where your level of privacy protection was when you first started reading this guide compared to where you've elevated it to now. This is because you've implemented a thorough security strategy.

There is so much about information technology and the online world that many everyday users need help understanding. Much of that lack of knowledge stems from so many resources that it can be overwhelming.

We have gone to great lengths to make fundamental cybersecurity information accessible and easily understandable for everyone. Our end goal is to create a safer digital environment for everyone by sharing knowledge in layperson's terms and not leaving anyone feeling excluded, even if they're not particularly tech-savvy.

By taking your cyber privacy and protection seriously, you have increased your own information protection, and you also taken a step toward thwarting cybercriminals the world over. And by leaving an honest review of your experience of following this guide, you can help others do the same, ultimately spreading awareness and knowledge that will help build a safer cyber world for everyone.

Please visit the following link or scan the QR code to leave feedback on Amazon.

https://www.amazon.com/review/create-review/?asin= 1738431207

CONCLUSION

Effective cybersecurity practices are vital for anyone navigating this life which has today become inextricably intertwined with information technology. While some aspects might seem straightforward, the knowledge necessary to safeguard yourself from cyber attacks isn't simple. It's therefore important that you know the best practices and protocols to keep your privacy safe. It's invaluable knowledge and a crucial skill set that anyone can and should prioritize learning.

Most of this guide has focused on how to improve your own cybersecurity, but it's also highlighted some pertinent broader concepts. Your cybersecurity affects the security of others, especially when you know, possess, or communicate sensitive or valuable information about the people you know. Similarly, the people you know can influence your cybersecurity based on what information they know, possess, or communicate about you. As such, effective cybersecurity for individuals is a concerted group effort to gain the knowledge and skills as well as implement the best practices necessary to protect the information of yourself and others.

This guide has provided all the necessary fundamental concepts, practices, and tools to educate you about the importance and impact of cybersecurity. By understanding the tools and measures required for cybersecurity, you now know:

- What cybersecurity is
- Why it's important
- What the impact of security or data breaches are
- What a cybersecurity strategy is, and what it should include
- The ethics and legalities surrounding cybersecurity and their value for protecting consumers like you and your nearest and dearest

Additionally, the step-by-step guide has walked you through:

- Securing your devices and networks
- Improving online browsing safety measures
- Creating and implementing strong login credentials and safer authentication
- Basic cyber hygiene practices
- How to navigate social media more safely

You are now equipped with the tools and knowledge you need to start securing every aspect of your digital life and minimize your vulnerability to cybercriminals. Even the tightest cybersecurity strategy and measures aren't infallible. However, having a proper, thorough strategy that utilizes vital protocols and tools leaves you far less vulnerable to cybercrime and dramatically reduces the chances of an attack's success.

Cybercrime is continually evolving alongside the ever-changing technology it's meant to exploit. It's imperative to keep yourself updated with cybercrime trends to ensure that your knowledge and safety measures don't become outdated or develop weak points in your cybersecurity. Start implementing your own cybersecurity strategy today and remember to revisit it regularly. Perform audits that will repair security vulnerabilities and maintain your security integrity. Whenever you do a cybersecurity audit, take advantage of the Cybersecurity Master Checklist to streamline your security checks. As we close this journey through the world of cybersecurity, remember that your proactive steps in safeguarding your digital life are not just a one-time effort, but a continuous journey towards a safer digital existence. The knowledge you've gained is a powerful tool in this ever-evolving digital age. Embrace the challenge with confidence, knowing that each step you take enhances not only your own security but contributes to a safer digital world for everyone. Let this book be a starting point, a guide that empowers you to navigate the digital landscape with awareness and resilience. Your journey in cybersecurity is a testament to your commitment to adapt and thrive in the digital era. Keep learning, stay vigilant, and remember, in the vast expanse of the digital universe, you are not just a user; you are a guardian of your own digital frontier.

GLOSSARY

Anti-malware: Software designed to guard devices and networks against malicious attacks.

Anti-phishing: Software designed to safeguard users from phishing attacks by identifying suspicious emails and blocking access to phishing websites.

Antivirus: Software specifically designed to detect common virus attacks and some malware attacks. Antivirus software should be complemented with anti-malware for increased protection.

Authentication: A process of identifying and verifying that a user is authorized to access a device, system, network, application, account, or some other form of information or communication.

Brute force attack: The process of bombarding an authentication portal with a large volume of password combinations, or encryption key combinations, until the correct login credentials are found.

Cryptomining: Cybercriminals employing unsuspecting users' compromised devices to generate cryptocurrency without their knowledge or consent. The device's performance degenerates due to the computing power being redirected to the "mining" efforts. The process is also known as cryptojacking.

Cybersecurity: The practices used and measures taken to secure information within devices, systems, networks, accounts, and other forms of information storage and communications.

Dark web: Parts of the internet that are encrypted and not indexed by search engines. It is most commonly used for nefarious purposes by a wide range of criminals. Activity is challenging to trace, and criminals hide behind anonymity, encryption access control, and peer-to-peer network connections.

Data breach: When a cybercriminal successfully gains unauthorized access to sensitive information by exploiting the vulnerabilities of humans, devices, networks, and software.

Data integrity: The quality, accuracy and consistency of data. Data integrity is a broad "umbrella" term with different meanings in different contexts. Data integrity is all about maintaining information accuracy and consistency for the duration of the data's lifespan. This means that it should not be changed in a way that is unauthorized, is transmitted in a reliable way, and is stored securely.

Data theft: The theft of information by cybercriminals for malicious purposes.

DoS and DDoS: Denial of Service (DoS) attacks use one device to flood a targeted system with requests, resulting in the system becoming overloaded and unable to service legitimate customers, thereby disrupting the provision of service. Distributed Denial of Service (DDoS) attacks utilize multiple devices to carry out a DoS attack.

Decryption: Decoding encrypted data to render it "readable".

Encryption: Converting data into "unreadable" code that requires a decryption key to decrypt the scrambled or encoded data, in order to make it "readable" again.

Exploit: The process of taking advantage of a flaw or vulnerability to gain unauthorized access and execute a malicious attack.

Firewall: A hardware or software security tool that creates a virtual barrier between devices and the internet, in order to prevent hackers and malicious programs from accessing your data.

Hacker: A person who attempts to gain unauthorized access to devices, systems, or networks, usually for criminal purposes. Ethical hackers perform the same attacks as a service in order to assist legitimate organizations, in a bid to uncover vulnerabilities and improve security.

Identity theft: The accessing of and gathering of information about a user, in order to enable criminals to impersonate their victim for malicious purposes. Stolen identities can be used for various crimes, including stealing goods or services, fraudulently opening bank accounts or lines of credit, holding accounts for ransom, and more.

Intrusion Detection System (IDS): A security measure designed to detect unauthorized access to information.

Intrusion Detection and Prevention System (IDPS): A security measure designed to detect and prevent unauthorized access.

Intrusion Prevention System (IPS): A security measure designed to prevent unauthorized access.

IoT: The Internet of Things refers to machines and devices connected to the internet. The vast array of technology in the IoT includes smartphones, smart watches, household appliances, and CCTV cameras.

Keylogger: Spyware, which is a type of malware, designed to record each keystroke made on a device. A Keylogger is used to gather information such as conversations and login credentials.

Malware: Any program designed for malicious purposes to cause harm to technology users.

Man-in-the-middle attack (MITM): Attacks where data is intercepted while it's in transit between two points to gather sensitive information.

Password spraying: One common password is used by cybercriminals to log into multiple accounts on the same application in the hope that one of the accounts will have that password. Password spraying avoids account lockouts, which can occur with brute force attacks.

Patch: Updated or revised operating system code, or application code, to improve potential vulnerabilities, usually delivered in updates.

Personally identifiable information (PII): Any information that might be used to ascertain the identity of an individual.

Phishing: A cyberattack in which victims are encouraged to provide sensitive information that can be used to access accounts. Attacks can be messages, emails, malicious pop-ups, or even phone calls.

Ransomware: A type of malware designed to withhold data or block access to devices, accounts, networks, or systems until a ransom is paid to regain access. Some ransomware developers attempt to impersonate law enforcement to improve the perceived credibility of their scam.

Sandboxing: A security measure where a sandbox or isolated digital space is used to run potentially suspicious programs. Programs infected with malicious code are safely contained without putting the device or network at risk.

Scareware: A type of malware which tricks users into clicking on malicious links by giving them a false warning, such as the device being infected with a virus.

Sniffing: Packet sniffing captures data in transit between two points. It can be used for either security or malicious purposes. Unencrypted data is at risk of being gathered and used in cybercrime.

Social engineering: Criminal attacks based on human behavior and psychology to manipulating victims into divulging information.

Spam: Messages or emails received without user's consent. This "junk mail" may often be part of phishing attacks.

Spear phishing: Phishing attacks explicitly targeting a particular individual or organization.

Spoofing: Digital impersonation that can take many forms, including impersonating a legitimate user to gain unauthorized access, using false communication details such as email addresses or phone numbers, or luring users to fake websites that mimic their legitimate counterparts.

Spyware: A type of malware that secretly gathers data or information about user activity and relays it to cyber-criminals.

Threat assessment: The process of identifying risks and evaluating current security measures for vulnerabilities.

Two-factor authentication (2FA): This is an authentication process utilizing two separate methods to verify that a user is authorized to access data.

Virtual Private Network (VPN): A private network that uses encryption to act as a secure channel of communication over a shared or public network (the internet).

Virus: A malicious program that can perform one or several harmful actions that damage a device, system, or network, a data breach, or hijacking a device, system, or network.

Vulnerability: A weakness in a program, system, or network that can be exploited by cybercriminals to gain unauthorized access to data, devices, systems, or networks.

White hat (and black hat): Terms used to describe and differentiate between ethical and unethical behavior. White hat practices fall within legal codes of conduct, while black hat practices are illegal.

Free Cybersecurity Course!

Jumpstart your journey to a safer digital world! Sign up now for our exciting, free course on cybersecurity!

Cybersecurity Unlocked: A 10-Email Masterclass in Cybersecurity Essentials

- Master cybersecurity and safeguard your digital identity with our step-by-step guide!
- Dive into interactive lessons, quizzes, and real-world scenarios
- Gain expert insights on common online threats and practical tools to secure your devices and personal info

To get your free course, please visit the link or scan the QR code below and let us know the email address to send it to.

pages.techedpublishers.com/bonus/cpntu

Don't miss out!

REFERENCES

10 personal cyber security tips - #CyberAware. (2017, October 29). Cypher. https://cipher.com/blog/10-personal-cyber-security-tips-cyberaware/

100+ cybersecurity terms & definitions you should know. (n.d.). Allot. https://www.allot.com/100-plus-cybersecurity-terms-definitions/

7 ways to protect my online accounts. (n.d.). What Is My IP. https://www.whatismyip.com/protect-online-accounts/

A holistic approach to ethical issues in cyber security. (2021, March 19). Swiss Cyber Institute. https://swisscyberinstitute.com/blog/a-holistic-approach-to-ethical-issues-in-cyber-security/

Aggan, W. (n.d.). *How cybersecurity affects legal ethics compliance.* Cloudmask. https://www.cloudmask.com/blog/how-cybersecurity-affects-legal-ethics-compliance

Baker, K. (2023, February 13). *10 most common types of cyber attacks.* Crowd-Strike. https://www.crowdstrike.com/cybersecurity-101/cyberattacks/most-common-types-of-cyberattacks

Best practices for backup plans. (n.d.). MSP360. https://help.mspbackups.com/security/security-best-practices/best-practices-for-backup-plans

Brithny., & Cici. (2023, July 20). *How to permanently delete files from computer without recovery Windows 11/10/8/7.* EaseUS. https://www.easeus.com/partition-manager-software/permanently-delete-files-from-computer-without-recovery.html

Can I teach myself cyber security? (2020, December 17). Security Made Simple. https://www.securitymadesimple.org/cybersecurity-blog/can-i-teach-myself-cybersecurity

Chachak, E. (2022, April 6). *How to keep your backup data secure.* Cyber DB. https://www.cyberdb.co/how-to-keep-your-backup-data-secure/

Chin, K.l (2023, July 18). *Biggest data breaches in US history (updated 2023).* UpGuard. https://www.upguard.com/blog/biggest-data-breaches-us

Chipeta, C. (2022, August 18). *What is the cyber threat landscape?* UpGuard. https://www.upguard.com/blog/cyber-threat-landscape

Clean Email Team. (2023, July 14). *Most secure email provider 2023.* Clean

Email. https://clean.email/blog/email-security/most-secure-email-provider

Cobb, M. (20o21, July). *How to perform a cybersecurity risk assessment in 5 steps.* Tech Target. https://www.techtarget.com/searchsecurity/tip/How-to-perform-a-cybersecurity-risk-assessment-step-by-step

Code injection in brief: Types, examples, and mitigation. (2022, January 31). Bright Security. https://brightsec.com/blog/code-injection/

Complete guide to cyber risk assessments. (2023, February 13). RiskOptics. https://reciprocity.com/resources/complete-guide-to-cyber-risk-assessments/

Cordiner, S. (2022, June 9). *14 ways to protect your intellectual properly (online curse videos & content).* Thinkific. https://www.thinkific.com/blog/intellectual-property-online-courses/

Cordiner, S. (2022, June 9). *What is intellectual property and why does it matter for course creators?* Thinkific. https://www.thinkific.com/blog/intellectual-property-online-courses/#what-is

Crail, C. (2023, February 9). *VPN statistics and trends in 2023.* Forbes Advisor. https://www.forbes.com/advisor/business/vpn-statistics/

Cybersecurity best practices. (n.d.). Cybersecurity and Infrastructure Security Agency CISA. https://www.cisa.gov/topics/cybersecurity-best-practices

Cybersecurity: Tips and tricks to stay vigilant. (n.d.). The Personal. https://www.thepersonal.com/blog/-/cybersecurity-tips-and-tricks-to-stay-vigilant

Data backup in depth: Concepts, techniques, and storage technologies. (n.d.). Cloudian. https://cloudian.com/guides/data-backup/data-backup-in-depth/

De Groot, J. (2022, December 21). *101 data protection tips: How to keep your passwords, financial & personal information online safe.* Digital Guardian. https://www.digitalguardian.com/de/blog/101-data-protection-tips-how-keep-your-passwords-financial-personal-information-online-safe

Dehoyos, M. (2019, August 2). *10 ways to remain vigilant against cyberattacks.* United States Cybersecurity Magazine. https://www.uscybersecurity.net/10-ways-to-remain-vigilant-against-cyberattacks/

DePrisco, F. (2023, February 15). *Cybersecurity laws and legislation (2023).* Connectwise. https://www.connectwise.com/blog/cybersecurity/cybersecurity-laws-and-legislation

Deshpande, C. (2022, November 18). *What is firewall: Types, how does it work, advantages & its importance.* Simplilearn. https://www.simplilearn.com/tutorials/cyber-security-tutorial/what-is-firewall

Drapkin, A. (2023, July 27). *Data breaches that have happened in 2022 and 2023 so far.* Tech.co. https://tech.co/news/data-breaches-updated-list

Ensuring cybersecurity with cookies: Best practices and tips. (n.d.) Devoteam. https://www.devoteam.com/expert-view/cybersecurity-cookies/

Ethical issues in cybersecurity. (n.d.). Comp TIA's Future of Tech. https://www.futureoftech.org/cybersecurity/4-ethical-issues-in-cybersecurity/

Everything you need to know b out hard drive destruction. (2023, January 30). Securis. https://securis.com/news/everything-you-need-to-know-about-hard-drive-destruction/

Farrelly, J. (2022, January 12). *Anti malware vs. antivirus: Definitions and differences.* Electric. https://www.electric.ai/blog/anti-malware-vs-antivirus

Fichtner, E. (2022, January 31). *Common types of cyber attacks.* Datto Security Solutions. https://www.datto.com/blog/common-types-of-cyber-security-attacks

Frankenfield, J. (2022, February 11). *What is an eavesdropping attack?* Investopedia. https://www.investopedia.com/terms/e/eavesdropping-attack.asp

Goldstein, P. (2023, March 31). *DNS tunnelling and DNS spoofing: How federal agencies can mount a defense.* FedTech. https://fedtechmagazine.com/article/2022/03/dns-tunneling-and-dns-spoofing-how-federal-agencies-can-mount-defense-perfcon

Griffith, E., & Steele, C. (2020, August 19). *How to control and delete cookies on your browser.* PC Mag. https://www.pcmag.com/how-to/how-to-control-and-delete-cookies-on-your-browser

Griffiths, C. (2023, October 2). The Latest 2023 Cybercrime Statistics. AAG. https://aag-it.com/the-latest-cyber-crime-statistics/

Hall, A. (2023, July 28). *How to protect intellectual property in 5 different ways.* Copyrighted. https://www.copyrighted.com/blog/protect-intellectual-property

Haman, E. (2023, May 11). *Understanding digital rights management.* Legal Zoom. https://www.legalzoom.com/articles/understanding-digital-rights-management#copyrights-and-drm

Harvey, S. (2020, March 5). *Stay secure with these intrusion detection and* protection techniques. Kirkpatrick Price. https://kirkpatrickprice.com/blog/idps-techniques/

Hertzog, C. (2016, October 13). *You can't have privacy without security.* National

Cybersecurity Alliance. https://staysafeonline.org/cybersecurity-for-business/you-cant-have-privacy-without-security/

Hill, M., & Swinhoe, D. (2022, November 8). *The 15 biggest data breaches of the 21st century*. CSO Online. https://www.csoonline.com/article/2130877/the-biggest-data-breaches-of-the-21st-century.html

Hope for the best, prepare for the worst. (2022, February 3). Rising Kashmir. http://risingkashmir.com/-hope-for-the-best-prepare-for-the-worst

https://staysafeonline.org/cybersecurity-for-business/you-cant-have-privacy-without-security/

Huculak, M. (2022, October 5). *How to use BitLocker drive encryption on Windows 10*. Windows Central. https://www.windowscentral.com/how-use-bitlocker-encryption-windows-10

Ibeneme, C. (2022, December 12). *Host-based intrusion detection system: Definition, how it works, & threats guide*. Liquid Web. https://www.liquidweb.com/blog/host-based-intrusion-detection-system/

Ingalls, S. (2023, Janury 23). *13 best intrusion detection and prevention systems (IDPS) for 2023*. eSecurity Planet. https://www.esecurityplanet.com/products/intrusion-detection-and-prevention-systems/

Jennings, M. (2022, May 4). *Top data breaches and cyber attacks of 2022*. Tech Radar. https://www.techradar.com/features/top-data-breaches-and-cyber-attacks-of-2022

Klosowski, T. (2019). *How to protect your digital privacy*. The New York Times. https://www.nytimes.com/guides/privacy-project/how-to-protect-your-digital-privacy

Küçükkarakurt, F. (2022, October 27). *5 simple ways to improve your router and modem security*. Make Use Of. https://www.makeuseof.com/tips-securing-router-modem/

Lakhwani, S. (2023, July 14). *Fundamentals of cybersecurity (the basics guide)*. Knowledge Hut. https://www.knowledgehut.com/blog/security/cyber-security-fundamentals

Lees, H. (2022, February 26). *Hardware vs. software firewalls: A guide for SMBWs in 2022*. Trust Radius. https://www.trustradius.com/buyer-blog/hardware-vs-software-firewalls

Lynch, H, & Hanna, J. (2019, September 14). An Ohio gamer gets prison time over a 'swatting' call that led to a man's death. CNN. https://edition.cnn.com/2019/09/14/us/swatting-sentence-casey-viner/index.html

Maintain good cybersecurity habits. (2023, April 3). Morgan Stanley. https://www.morganstanley.com/articles/personal-cybersecurity

Manyinsa, D. (2022, June 13). *6 key features to expect from secure email providers.* Make Use Of. https://www.makeuseof.com/features-from-the-most-secure-email-providers/

Marian, H. (2023, February 15). *Antivirus versus anti malware: Which one should you choose?* Heimdal Security. https://heimdalsecurity.com/blog/antivirus-vs-antimalware/

Marshall, KI. (2020, January 3). *Why do magnets wipe hard drives?* West Coast Computer Recycler. https://www.wcrecycler.com/blog/why-do-magnets-wipe-hard-drives

Melnick, J. (2023, March 17). *Top 10 most common types of cyber attacks.* Netwrix. https://blog.netwrix.com/2018/05/15/top-10-most-common-types-of-cyber-attacks/

Milich, A. (2023, February 26). *Email TSL encryption – what it is, and how much protection it offers.* Skiff. https://skiff.com/blog/email-tls-encryption

Modem vs router: What's the difference? (n.d.). Xfinity. https://www.xfinity.com/hub/internet/modem-vs-router

Mohanakrishnan, R. (2022, February 11). *What is intrusion detection and prevention system? Definition, examples, techniques and best practices.* Spiceworks. https://www.spiceworks.com/it-security/vulnerability-management/articles/what-is-idps/

Oza, S. (2022, August 1). *Backup encryption: What it is and why it's important.* Spanning. https://spanning.com/blog/backup-encryption/

Oza, S. (2022, August 1). *Backup encryption: What it is and why it's important for data security.* Spanning. https://spanning.com/blog/backup-encryption/

Pankaj, P. (2019, April 8). *Intrusion detection system (IDS).* GeeksforGeeks. https://www.geeksforgeeks.org/intrusion-detection-system-ids/

Pert, L. (2019, August 15). *Biometric security for businesses.* Open VPN. https://openvpn.net/blog/biometric-security-for-businesses/

Poggi, N. (2022, June 3). *Cybersecurity frameworks 101 – the complete guide.* Prey Project. https://preyproject.com/blog/cybersecurity-frameworks-101

Pourkhomami, P. (2023, January 19). *10 tips for making web browsing more secure.* OSIbeyond. https://www.osibeyond.com/blog/tips-for-making-web-browsing-more-secure/

Pourkhomami, P. (2023, January 19). *10 tips for making web browsing more secure.* OSIbeyond. https://www.osibeyond.com/blog/tips-for-making-web-browsing-more-secure/

Pradnya. (2022, March 10). *VPN security: How 2FA helps to secure your VPN?* Blog – MiniOrange. https://blog.miniorange.com/vpn-security-how-2fa-helps-to-secure-your-vpn/

Price, D. (2023, February 23). *Five eyes, nine eyes, and 14 eyes surveillance explained.* Make Use Of. https://www.makeuseof.com/tag/five-eyes-surveillance/

Proofpoint Staff. (2020, February 20). *5 good computer security habits.* Proof-point. https://www.proofpoint.com/us/blog/security-awareness-training/5-good-computer-security-habits

Sammon, M. (2022, June 18). *The importance of intellectual property protection.* Sonder & Clay. https://www.sonderandclay.com/ip-advice/the-importance-of-intellectual-property-protection/

SDO Marketing Staff. (2017, December 13). *Why your corporate VPN needs two-factor authentication (2FA).* Secret Double Octopus. https://doubleoctopus.com/blog/access-management/corporate-vpn-needs-two-factor-authentication-2fa/

Siege Media. (2023, May 11). How to protect your intellectual property. Legal Zoom. https://www.legalzoom.com/articles/how-to-protect-your-intellectual-property#strong-4-tips-for-protecting-intellectual-property-strong

Simplilearn Staff. (2023, February 14). *What is a cyber security framework: Types, benefits, & best practices.* Simplilearn. https://www.simplilearn.com/what-is-a-cyber-security-framework-article

Smith, N. (2018, June 13). *Firewall and IPS vs. NGFW: Which is the best for you?* Fortinet. https://www.fortinet.com/blog/business-and-technology/two-options-for-evolving-your-ips-solution

Stateful & stateless firewall differences. (n.d.). Fortinet. https://www.fortinet.com/resources/cyberglossary/stateful-vs-stateless-firewall

Straw, P. (n.d.). *6 habits for better cyber security.* GES. https://insights.ges.com/us-blog/6-habits-for-better-cybersecurity

Tackle cybersecurity with these must-have tools. (n.d.). Superscript. https://gosuperscript.com/news-and-resources/must-have-cyber-security-tools/

The increasing focus on cyber ethics issues. (2019, July 2). Maryville University. https://online.maryville.edu/blog/cyber-security-ethics/

The threat landscape. (n.d.). Encyclopedia Kaspersky. https://encyclopedia. kaspersky.com/glossary/threat-landscape/

Top 10 secure computing tips. (2019). Berkeley University of California. https:// security.berkeley.edu/resources/best-practices-how-to-articles/top-10-secure-computing-tips

Top 20 most common types of cyber attacks. (2023). Fortinet. https://www. fortinet.com/resources/cyberglossary/types-of-cyber-attacks

Tran, D. (2023, March 1). *Data breaches affecting millions of Australians are on the rise information commissioner says.* ABC News. https://www.abc.net.au/ news/2023-03-01/data-breaches-revealed-by-australian-information-commissioner/102039710

Trevino, A. (2023, March 9). *The importance of keeping software up to date.* Keeper Security. https://www.keepersecurity.com/blog/2023/03/09/the-importance-of-keeping-software-up-to-date/

Tunggal, A. (2023, July 18). *Why is cybersecurity important?* UpGuard. https:// www.upguard.com/blog/cybersecurity-important

Tunggal, A. (2023, June 29). *How to perform a cybersecurity risk assessment.* UpGuard. https://www.upguard.com/blog/cyber-security-risk-assessment

Vallor, S., & Rewak, W. (n.d.). An introduction to cybersecurity ethics. https://www.scu.edu/media/ethics-center/technology-ethics/ IntroToCybersecurityEthics.pdf

WAF vs. firewall: Web application & network firewalls. (n.d.). Fortinet. https:// www.fortinet.com/resources/cyberglossary/waf-vs-firewall

Walsh, R. (2021, March 11). *How to encrypt an external hard drive.* ProPrivacy. https://proprivacy.com/guides/encrypt-external-hard-drive

What is a cloud firewall? What is firewall-as-a-service (FWaaS)? (n.d.). Cloudflare. https://www.cloudflare.com/learning/cloud/what-is-a-cloud-firewall/

What is a hardware firewall? Hardware vs. software firewalls. (n.d.). Fortinet. https://www.fortinet.com/resources/cyberglossary/hardware-firewalls-better-than-software

What is a next-generation firewall (NGFW)? (n.d.). Cloudflare. https://www. cloudflare.com/learning/security/what-is-next-generation-firewall-ngfw/

What is a packet? | Network packet definition. (n.d.). Cloudflare. https://www. cloudflare.com/learning/network-layer/what-is-a-packet/

What is a spoofing attack? (n.d.). Malwarebytes. https://www.malwarebytes. com/spoofing

What is a stateful firewall? (n.d.). Fortinet. https://www.fortinet.com/resources/cyberglossary/stateful-firewall

What is a VPN and how does it work? (2020, November 3). Kaspersky. https://www.kaspersky.com/resource-center/definitions/what-is-a-vpn

What is bug bounty program? (2023, March 14). Intellipaat. https://intellipaat.com/blog/what-is-bug-bounty-program/?US

What is cybersecurity compliance? (n.d.). The Computing Technology Industry Association (CompTIA). https://www.comptia.org/content/articles/what-is-cybersecurity-compliance

What is cybersecurity risk analysis? (2022, August 18). RiskOptics. https://reciprocity.com/resources/what-is-cybersecurity-risk-analysis/

What is end-to-end encryption (E2EE)? (n.d.). Cloudflare. https://www.cloudflare.com/learning/privacy/what-is-end-to-end-encryption/

What is ethical hacking and how does it work? (n.d.). Synopsis. https://www.synopsys.com/glossary/what-is-ethical-hacking.html

What is IoT? (n.d.). Oracle. https://www.oracle.com/za/internet-of-things/what-is-iot/

What is proxy firewall and how does it work? (n.d.). Zenarmor. https://www.zenarmor.com/docs/network-security-tutorials/what-is-proxy-firewall

What should be considered when choosing a firewall?> (n.d.). Zenarmor. https://www.zenarmor.com/docs/network-security-tutorials/what-should-be-considered-when-choosing-a-firewall

Williamson, R. (2021, September 16). *Secure your devices: How to keep your computer and phone safe.* CIRA. https://www.cira.ca/blog/cybersecurity/how-to-secure-your-devices

Yadav, A. (2020, August 4). *Network design: Firewall, IDS/IPS.* Infotec Resources. https://resources.infosecinstitute.com/topic/network-design-firewall-idsips/

ABOUT THE AUTHOR

TechEd Publishers is dedicated to bringing reliable and useful information about technology to readers from all backgrounds. Our goal is to provide clear, factual education on technologies that can improve the way we live and work.

TechEd Publishers is made up of diverse and driven individuals who are passionate about using technology to improve quality of life. Our team members have a range of expertise and experience in business, technology, finance, work-life balance, and research. We are committed to making technological education accessible to anyone who wants to improve their own life and the lives of those around them. Our team's diversity is one of our greatest strengths, and what brings us together is our belief that technology can be used to improve the quality of life for everyone.

In addition to our focus on providing practical and actionable knowledge about technology, we also strive to inspire and motivate our readers to take advantage of the many ways that technology can enhance their lives. We believe that technology has the power to transform and improve the world we live in, and we are dedicated to sharing that message with as many people as possible.

Whether you are a business professional looking to stay up to date on the latest tech trends, a student interested in pursuing a career in technology, or just someone who wants to learn more about how technology can make your life easier and more efficient, TechEd Publishers has something to offer you. Our team members are experts in their respective fields, and we are confident their insights and advice will be valuable to anyone looking to make the most of the ever-evolving world of technology.

In addition to our focus on education, we also prioritize staying up-to-date on the latest tech developments and trends. We are always on the lookout for new technologies and innovations that have the potential to change the world, and we are dedicated to bringing our readers the latest news and insights about these exciting developments.

We believe that technology has the power to make a positive impact on the world, and we are committed to doing our part to help people understand and leverage the many benefits it has to offer.

Thank you for choosing TechEd Publishers as your source for reliable and informative technology education.

TechEd Publishers is the brand behind 'Video Making for Beginners and 'A Non-Techie Beginners' Guide to Cybersecurity and Privacy'.

facebook.com/techedpublishers
instagram.com/techedpublishers
amazon.com/author/techedpublishers

ALSO BY TECHED PUBLISHERS

Video Making for Beginners: Discover the Proven Techniques Used by Pros to Create High-Quality Professional Videos for Less Cost and in Less Time Even Without Experience

Whether you're tasked with a work presentation, a webinar, or social media content, this book will reveal the proven techniques used by experts to create high-quality professional videos for any project - and turn the amateur video maker into a pro!

www.ingramcontent.com/pod-product-compliance
Lightning Source LLC
La Vergne TN
LVHW092010050326
832904LV00002B/43